Drugs and Crime in Lifestyle Perspective

Drugs, Health, and Social Policy Series

Edited by James A. Inciardi

About This Series . . .

The Sage Drugs, Health, and Social Policy Series provides students and professionals in the fields of substance abuse, AIDS, public health, and criminal justice access to current research, programs, and policy issues particular to their specialties. Each year, four new volumes will focus on a topic of national significance.

1. **Drugs and Crime in Lifestyle Perspective**
   Glenn D. Walters

Drugs and Crime in Lifestyle Perspective

Glenn D. Walters

Drugs, Health, and Social Policy Series
Volume I

SAGE Publications
International Educational and Professional Publisher
Thousand Oaks   London   New Delhi

For information address:

SAGE Publications, Inc.
2455 Teller Road
Thousand Oaks, California 91320

SAGE Publications Ltd.
6 Bonhill Street
London EC2A 4PU
United Kingdom

SAGE Publications India Pvt. Ltd.
M-32 Market
Greater Kailash I
New Delhi 110 048 India

Printed in the United States of America

Library of Congress Cataloging-in-Publication Data

Walters, Glenn D.
    Drugs and crime in lifestyle perspective / author, Glenn D. Walters.
        p.   cm.—(Drugs, health, and social policy; 1)
    Includes bibliographical references and index.
    ISBN 0-8039-5601-0 (cl).—ISBN 0-8039-5602-9 (pb)
    1. Drug abuse—Government policy—United States. 2. Drug abuse and crime—United States. 3. Drug abuse—United States—Prevention. 4. Drug abuse—Treatment—United States. I. Title. II. Series.
    HV5825.W381264   1994
    364.2'4—dc20   93-46438

94 95 96 97 98   10 9 8 7 6 5 4 3 2 1

Sage Production Editor: Yvonne Könneker

Contents

Preface

Drugs and crime have long held the fascination of the American public. Although the negative consequences of drug use and criminal activity have been extensively documented, the reader may be surprised to learn that these problems are not of recent onset. Even before the American Revolution, life in America was periodically disrupted by the machinations of highway robbers and the irrational behavior of persons acting under the influence of intoxicating beverages. It is therefore imperative that we do not overinterpret the current situation with respect to drug use and crime, but rather work to balance present-day concerns about drug-seeking behavior and crime with the realization that these problems are well ingrained in the American experience. In the pages that follow, I will present sundry perspectives on drug abuse, crime, and their interrelationship in an effort to ascertain the true nature of the drug-crime connection across specific conditions, situations, and circumstances. The first order of business, however, concerns the clarification of terms such as *drug abuse* and *crime*.

A *drug* is normally defined as any chemical substance other than food that affects the structure or function of the body. I restrict the present investigation to chemical compounds capable of altering a person's mood or subjective emotional state—alcohol, marijuana, cocaine, and heroin, among others. Whether a drug is legal or illegal, manufactured or harvested, injected or swallowed, what is of prime significance is that the substance lends itself to widespread misuse because of its mood-altering properties. Though the drug-crime connection may vary as a function of specific drugs used or crimes committed, my focus in the present discussion will be on the more general relationship presumed to exist between drugs of abuse and criminal outcome. Hence, in referencing drugs, the definition will be restricted to common drugs of abuse, *drug abuse* being defined as the regular or habitual use of one or more of these substances to the point where the individual suffers multiple major life problems as a consequence.

Identifying a useful definition of *crime* also presents problems for scholars interested in probing the drug-crime connection, because the correlates of crime frequently vary as a function of the definition employed. Definitions of crime run the gamut from highly behavioral conceptualizations, such as those employed by research psychologists, to the legal definitions adopted by the judiciary and the criminal justice system. In this text I will attempt to merge these two trends by defining crime as rule-breaking behavior that, if known to legal authorities, would result in the rule breaker's being charged with a criminal offense punishable by law. Whether this law-violating behavior occurs during adolescence or adulthood is less important than documenting the rule-violating nature of the behavior and certifying that the individual was cognizant of the wrongfulness of his or her actions at the time the offense was committed. Though such a definition may appear overly inclusive to some, it nonetheless succeeds in capturing the legal foundation of many commonly accepted definitions of criminality.

A perspective can be conceived of as one's manner of viewing a particular event, situation, or issue. In the chapters that follow, I will review and scrutinize data and perspectives relevant to the putative association between drug abuse and crime. There are, to be sure, many different perspectives potentially applicable to research on drug abuse, criminality, and their interconnection. In this book, I will examine several major categories of perspectives relevant to these concerns. To this end, I will explore condition-based, choice-based, and cognition-based viewpoints in an effort to construct a comprehensive explanation of the drug-crime connection. These perspectives offer behavioral scientists the opportunity to probe the boundaries and parameters of the drug-crime connection by allowing a structural appraisal of data pertinent to this relationship. With this in mind, let us turn our attention to the conditions, choices, cognitions, and change strategies viewed to be crucial in the development of drug and criminal lifestyles, and the overlap thought to exist between these two lifestyles.

Acknowledgments

I would like to express my deepest appreciation to my wife, Patti, and two children, Christopher and Tara, for the love, support, and patience they have demonstrated over the past year, without which this book never would have been possible.

The assertions and opinions contained herein are the private views of the author and should not be construed as official or as reflecting the views of the Federal Bureau of Prisons or the U.S. Department of Justice.

1. The Drug-Crime Connection

Newspapers, magazines, and television documentaries have chronicled the growing menace of drugs and crime in present-day American society and allude to the seeming futility of remedial efforts and interventions. Tales of drug abuse and crime are plastered across the front pages of local newspapers, dominate the evening news, and come to life in full-length cinematic productions and made-for-TV "movies of the week." The almost frenzied attention awarded drugs and crime by the national news media would appear to reflect a more generalized interest in such issues on the part of the American public. The task before us, then, is to identify a perspective or set of perspectives capable of advancing our knowledge on the origins, development, and treatment implications of the overlap presumed to exist between drug abuse and crime. Our search logically begins with investigations assessing the possibility of a meaningful statistical link between substance abuse and criminal outcome.

Before we can conclude that a causal nexus exists between two or more variables, we must first demonstrate that these variables are correlated or connected in some way. The putative drug-crime relationship has been investigated using both self-report and official measures of criminal conduct. A self-report survey of approximately 3,000 junior and senior high school students, for instance, revealed the presence of a significant correlation between substance abuse and non-drug-related delinquent activity (Akers, 1984). In a second study, urine analysis of arrestees in 24 U.S. cities uncovered one or more illegal substances in the specimens of 36%-75% of the tested males and 45%-79% of the tested females (O'Neil, 1992). The research methods most commonly employed in studies investigating the drug-crime connection, however, consider the drug-related self-reports of prison inmates and the recorded criminal activity of identified substance abusers.

Researchers who have studied drug use patterns in criminal populations report a relatively high rate of alcohol and/or illegal drug abuse in this population. Interviews conducted with a group of male delinquents housed in a Texas youth facility, for instance, disclosed that 40%-47% of the variation in minor delinquency and 34%-59% of the variation in violent delinquency could be credited to the subjects' use of legal and illegal substances (Watts & Wright, 1990). A large-scale national survey of alcohol use patterns in state prison inmates identified a history of daily alcohol abuse in 20% of the sample, with one in three inmates reporting that he was under the influence of alcohol at the time of the commission of the confining offense (Bureau of Justice Statistics, 1983a). In this same survey, two out of five state inmates acknowledged recent daily usage of an illegal substance and one in three reported having been under the influence of an illegal drug when committing the confining offense (Bureau of Justice Statistics, 1983b). As a substantial number of alcohol-abusing felons abstained from illegal drug use and a somewhat smaller percentage of drug-involved offenders did not drink, these results demonstrate that the majority of inmates surveyed had misused alcohol, illicit drugs, or both.

Studies scrutinizing the criminal activities of persons enrolled in substance abuse treatment programs indicate the presence of a vigorous and potentially meaningful connection between drug abuse and crime. Goodwin, Crane, and Guze (1971), for instance, compared the arrest records of problem and nonproblem drinkers and observed a significantly higher rate of arrest in the problem drinking group, though many of these arrests were for public intoxication, drunk driving, and other alcohol-related offenses. Probing the interlinkage of heroin addiction and crime, Eckerman, Bates, Rachal, and

Poole (1971) determined that 45%-80% of the arrests for robbery in Washington, D.C., and New York City, respectively, were of persons who either used or were dependent on heroin. The scope of the problem is clearly captured in Inciardi's (1979) report on 356 heroin addicts living in Miami, Florida; his conservative estimate is that these addicts committed 118,134 felonies during a one-year period.

The presence of an association between drugs and crime would seem self-evident; explaining this relationship, however, is somewhat more problematic. For instance, although drug use may cause crime under one set of conditions, criminal involvement may cause, or at least facilitate, drug use under a completely different set of conditions. These two possibilities fall into the category of unidirectional interpretations of the drug-crime relationship, in which drug abuse is seen as causing crime or crime is seen as causing drug abuse. A third possibility is that drugs and crime enjoy a reciprocal relationship—that is, the effects of drugs on crime and crime on drugs are bidirectional (drugs $\longleftrightarrow$ crime) rather than unidirectional (i.e., drugs $\rightarrow$ crime or drugs $\leftarrow$ crime). Finally, there are those who would argue that the observed association between drugs and crime is illusory and owes its existence to the action of a third variable with which both drugs and crime are correlated. A brief review of these four explanatory hypotheses may be of some use in an attempt to identify key elements of the drug-crime connection; such a review is therefore the next order of business.

Perhaps the most popular interpretation of the drug-crime correlation is that drugs cause crime. One way by which this particular hypothesis might be realized is through the direct effect of certain chemical substances on a person's judgment, self-control, or ability to inhibit violent impulses. All one need do is turn on the television or leaf through the pages of a local newspaper to find "evidence" in support of this exegesis of the drug-crime connection. The drugs-cause-violence hypothesis also receives support from several research studies that have found a substantial portion of all assaults and murders to be drug-related (Goldstein, 1986). However, although there is some indication that alcohol inebriation may facilitate the commission of specific criminal acts (Green, 1981), there is little consistent evidence in favor of a relationship between violence and the use of certain mind-altering substances—namely, cocaine (Carr & Meyers, 1980) and phencyclidine (PCP) (Brecher, Wang, Wong, & Morgan, 1988).

Another possibility is that the high cost of some illegal drugs precipitates criminality in those who are addicted to these substances.

Some 90% of the property offenders in New South Wales (Australia) prisons who reported regular use of heroin acknowledged having engaged in crime as a means of supporting their heroin habits (Dobinson & Ward, 1986). Along similar lines, Votey (1986) ascertained a substantial correlation between substance abuse and economically motivated crime but little relationship between substance abuse and violent crime. Longitudinal surveys of heroin addicts living in Baltimore, Maryland (Ball, Rosen, Flueck, & Nurco, 1981), Southern California (Anglin & Speckart, 1988), and Great Britain (Jarvis & Parker, 1989) also support a drugs-cause-crime interpretation of the drug-crime connection, in that economically oriented crime was heaviest during peak periods of opiate use and lightest during periods of abstinence. There would appear to be preliminary support, then, for the notion that the high cost of certain illegal substances may motivate persons to engage in crime as a means of supporting their growing dependency on drugs.

Owing to the fact that participation in the drug trade may breed violence independent of the direct physical or financial effects of drug abuse, it is conceivable that drug involvement could cause crime because of the violence found in the drug business. McBride, Burgman-Habermehl, Alpert, and Chitwood (1986) report that nearly one out of every four homicides occurring in Dade County, Florida, between 1978 and 1982 could be attributed to a conflict over the importation, distribution, or sale of an illegal substance. Given that many drug users are at least tangentially involved in the drug distribution "business," it may be that the violence previously ascribed to substance abuse may actually be more appropriately attributed to the violent nature of the drug trade. In a like manner, the use of illegal drugs may bring previously law-abiding (except for their use of illicit substances) individuals into contact with the criminal element and contribute to a gradual wearing down of these persons' moral codes and respect for the laws of society.

Behavioral scientists opting for a crime-causes-drug-abuse interpretation of the drug-crime connection highlight research intimating that crime and delinquency frequently predate substance abuse. This has been observed in persons who abuse alcohol (Nathan, 1988), heroin (Parker & Newcombe, 1987), and other drugs (Walters & White, 1987). Three possible scenarios suggest themselves with respect to the crime-causes-drug-abuse hypothesis. First, criminals sometimes use drugs as a prelude to crime. In support of this supposition, studies show that alcohol and other drugs may act to eliminate fear, apprehension, and other deterrents to criminal action

(Cromwell, Olson, Avary, & Marks, 1991). Second, offenders may use drugs as an expression of their hedonistic, self-indulgent approach to life (Walters, 1990) or as part of the celebration following a successful criminal venture (Gibbs & Shelly, 1982). Third, it has been noted that heroin addicts who have successfully maintained themselves on low-moderate doses of heroin will often raise their levels of usage when given access to a large influx of ready cash as a result of their participation in lucrative criminal acts (Faupel, 1987).

A third possible interpretation of the drug-crime relationship is that drugs and crime enjoy a reciprocal or bidirectional causal relationship (i.e., each variable is conceived to be a cause of the other), a possibility that finds support in a recent survey of 254 youth involved in the crack trade in Miami, Florida (Inciardi & Pottieger, 1991). The prospect of overlapping lifestyles for crime (Walters, 1990) and drug abuse (Walters, 1992a) is another example of how a reciprocal theory of drug-crime effects might be envisioned. Terrence Thornberry (1987) advocates greater use of reciprocal influence models in research delving into the origins of crime and delinquency. In so doing, Thornberry takes current criminological theories to task for failing to consider the possibility that delinquency may be as much a cause of such social problems and conditions as poor family communication, inadequate school achievement, and drug abuse as a consequence of these same social conditions. I will elaborate upon and examine the reciprocal influence hypothesis in much greater detail in subsequent chapters of this book, in an attempt to construct a lifestyle model of the drug-crime connection.

A fourth possible interpretation of drug-crime data is the "third-variable" explanation, which states that the drug-crime connection owes its existence to the presence of one or more additional variables with which both drug abuse and crime are correlated. This third variable is often left unspecified by proponents of this argument, although several possibilities suggest themselves. One explanation holds that general deviance artificially links drug abuse and crime because of its common association with both variables. Other variables potentially capable of serving this linking function include self-indulgence, social disaffection, and legal-political factors. Cross-indexing measures of drug abuse and crime in a large sample of juvenile offenders, Fagan, Weis, and Cheng (1990) observed results that led them to conclude that drugs and crime operate along parallel dimensions, but are not causally linked. The essence of the third-variable interpretation of the drug-crime connection is that there is no intrinsic or meaningful bond between drug abuse and crime other than that provided by their common association with some third variable.

The controversial nature of drug-crime research has helped spawn an attitude of entrenchment wherein the major schools of thought on the drug-crime connection have failed to consider the possibility that more than one explanation may be correct. Scanning the research literature in this area, one can find evidence in support of each of the four primary interpretations of drug-crime correlation (i.e., drugs → crime; crime → drugs; drugs ←→ crime; drugs ≠ crime), although disconfirmatory findings can also be identified for each model. Perhaps the most parsimonious interpretation of drug-crime data at this point in time is that the relationship between these two variables may assume any one of four versions depending on a collection of factors and additional considerations. Accordingly, there are certain drugs that, because of either their high cost or their violence-promoting qualities, cause specific criminal outcomes. At other times, however, a criminal offender may imbibe drugs to advance criminal goals or a drug abuser may increase his or her level of substance intake as a direct result of participation in a lucrative criminal event. The reciprocal nature of the drug-crime connection must also not be overlooked, in that it may explain the drug-crime overlap under a third set of conditions. Finally, a fourth set of circumstances may give rise to an illusory correlation between drug abuse and crime because of their common association with a specified or unspecified third variable.

From the perspective of the lifestyle theory of human decision making, drug abuse and criminal activity are conceived of as interrelated lifestyles, and the drug-crime connection is seen as falling within the overlap that exists between these two lifestyles. A *lifestyle* is defined by three interrelated influences, referred to in lifestyle theory as the "three Cs": conditions, choice, and cognition. Conditions, whether internal (heredity, temperament) or external (family, peers), positive (protective factors) or negative (risk factors), influence a person's future propensity to use drugs and engage in various criminal acts by affecting his or her range of life options. According to lifestyle theory, conditions do not cause drug abuse or crime in any direct sense, though they do influence these behaviors by increasing (protective factors) or decreasing (risk factors) a person's options in life. Once the conditional parameters have been established, the individual makes a choice or series of choices from the options available. The third C, cognition, evolves from a person's efforts to justify and rationalize the decisions he or she has made in life. The three Cs serve as the core components of a drug or criminal lifestyle, and it is the interacting network of influences created by these three features that gives birth to a lifestyle in which serious drug abuse or criminal activity assumes center stage.

In deriving treatment strategies useful in effecting change in someone committed to a drug or criminal lifestyle, lifestyle theory introduces a fourth C: change. It is proposed that change is possible and most effective if directed at the original three Cs, namely, the conditions, choices, and cognitions that reinforce and support a drug or criminal lifestyle. Condition-based intervention techniques are designed to assist clients in the management of various life conditions by limiting their access to drug and criminal activities, or by assisting them in the identification of a prosocial network of friends and acquaintances. Choice-based change strategies consider ways in which a person's options in life might be enhanced and his or her decision-making competence improved, whereas cognition-based intervention is directed at the cognitive patterns that support a drug or criminal lifestyle. The purpose of this book is to describe the drug and criminal lifestyles and demonstrate how the drug-crime connection can be ascribed, at least in part, to the overlap that exists between these two lifestyles.

2. Conditions

Conditions are features of the Person, Situation, or Person × Situation interaction that influence the probability of a future or concurrent behavioral outcome or event. In reviewing traditional models of drug abuse and crime, it becomes clear that conditions serve as the foundation for most such theories. Though undoubtedly not something to be ignored, conditions are but one feature of the equation employed by lifestyle theory to elucidate drug abuse, crime, and the drug-crime connection. The reader should also be aware that there are two general categories of conditional influence: historical-developmental conditions, which serve to increase or decrease a person's future risk of drug or criminal involvement, and current-contextual conditions, which influence the probability of a concurrent drug use or criminal event. Below, I discuss each of these two classes of conditions with respect to its person (characteristics of the individual), situation (characteristics of the environment), and interactive (characteristics of the Person × Situation interaction) subcomponents.

Historical-Developmental Conditions

Person Variables

Historical-developmental person variables are individual-level conditions such as age, heredity, autonomic response, and personality that influence the future probability of a drug or criminal outcome.

Age

Age is an important correlate of both drug use and crime. Hirschi and Gottfredson (1983) have chronicled the impact of aging on criminal offending, whereas others have done much the same with alcohol (e.g., Fillmore, 1988; Grant, Harford, & Grigson, 1988). Cross-sectional arrest data show that property crimes rise sharply during mid-adolescence (ages 14-16) and then drop just as sharply after age 16 or 17, whereas person-oriented crimes exhibit a flatter slope, peaking in early adulthood (ages 18-21) and following a more gradual decline than property offenses (Federal Bureau of Investigation, 1990). Longitudinal studies demonstrate comparable results with respect to the initiation and cessation of person-oriented and property crime (Shannon, 1982). Self-reported alcohol, marijuana, and polydrug use follows much the same pattern as crime, though the peak age of use (age 20) falls several years behind the peak age for general delinquency (Menard & Huizinga, 1989).

Hirschi and Gottfredson (1983) characterize the age-crime association as one of the brute facts of crime. The relationship between age and alcohol abuse is somewhat more controversial, owing to the fact that it tends to fluctuate in accordance with its definition. Cahalan and Room (1974), for instance, utilized three separate definitions of alcohol-related problems (binge drinking, interpersonal belligerence, and a record of police contact for drinking-related behavior) and discerned that although each behavior peaked in the youngest age group studied (21-24 years) and dropped to its lowest level in the older age group (40-59 years), the access and remission rates differed by definition. These findings intimate that drug abuse and crime follow similar age progressions and share many of the same age-related correlates. What this study fails to explain is whether the drug-crime bond for age is a function of an underlying connection between drugs and crime or simply a consequence of some unspecified third variable.

Heredity

The genetic correlates of drug abuse and crime have been investigated using data gathered from family, twin, and adoption studies. It has been inferred from the results of these studies that drug abuse and crime tend to run in families (Schuckit, 1987; Walters & White, 1989a). However, it is difficult to tease out the individual contributions of heredity and environment using the family method, and even the results of twin studies are open to question because they often confuse environmental and genetic influences. For this reason, adoption studies, in which the drug or criminal status of adoptees is compared with the drug or criminal status of their biological and adoptive parents, are seen as providing the strongest test of the genetic hypothesis. Outcomes derived from adoption studies reveal the presence of a small, but significant, genetic link for drug use (Cadoret, Troughton, O'Gorman, & Heywood, 1986) and crime (Mednick, Gabrielli, & Hutchings, 1984) that tends to be weaker in more recent and better-designed studies (Walters, 1992c).

The primary implication of behavioral genetic research is that substance abuse and crime appear to operate along divergent genetic lines, in that males demonstrate a stronger genetic effect for alcoholism and drug abuse (Pickens & Svikis, 1988), and females exhibit a slightly stronger genetic predisposition for crime (Lewis, Rice, & Helzer, 1983). The fact that Bohman, Cloninger, Sigvardsson, and von Knorring (1982) observed a significant adoptee-biological parent correlation for crime, but only in situations where the adoptee did not abuse alcohol, casts further doubt on the possibility of a common genetic link between drug abuse and crime. Likewise, Cadoret, O'Gorman, Troughton, and Heywood (1985) surmise that the heavy drinking they found in a group of American adoptees was predicted by parental and sibling alcohol abuse but not antisocial problems, whereas adoptee antisocial behavior was predicted by parental and sibling antisocial problems but not alcohol abuse. On the face of it, there would appear to be little evidence in support of the argument that the drug-crime connection is mediated by genetic factors.

Autonomic Response

An early study probing the effects of alcohol on autonomic functioning revealed the presence of a "normalizing" effect; alcohol enhanced sympathetic activity (increased heart rate, dilation of pupils, and so on) in persons with lower initial resting levels of sympathetic response and dampened sympathetic activity in persons with higher resting levels of sympathetic response (Kissin, Schenker, & Schenker, 1959). Finn and Pihl (1987) noted that sober subjects at risk for future alcohol abuse problems displayed greater cardio-vascular response (increased blood volume and heart rate) in antici-pation of a mild electrical shock than did sober moderate-risk or low-risk subjects. Furthermore, alcohol consumption led to de-creased physiological reactions in high-risk subjects but exerted a converse effect on moderate- and low-risk subjects. This suggests that subjects at risk for future alcohol abuse problems have a geneti-cally based hypersensitivity to stress that lessens with the introduc-tion of alcohol. Conversely, reduced sympathetic activity, as repre-sented by a slower-than-normal resting heart rate (Venables, 1987) and decreased skin conductance in response to stimulation (Ogloff & Wong, 1990), has been observed in persons who subsequently engage in criminal forms of behavior.

Although the observation that reduced autonomic response may be prognostic of delinquency in higher socioeconomic status (SES) samples (Venables et al., 1978), a plethora of fascinating possibili-ties suggest that autonomic functioning, which has clear genetic referents, may be a risk factor for crime in higher, but not lower, SES subjects, and there is little convincing proof that autonomic factors account for the drug-crime connection. In point of fact, research studies addressing this issue suggest that persons at risk for future drug abuse and criminal outcomes display antithetical auto-nomic response patterns, the former being characterized by auto-nomic hyperactivity and the latter by autonomic hypoactivity. In both cases, alcohol may produce a "normalizing" effect by decreas-ing or dampening the natural autonomic response of persons predis-posed to substance abuse and increasing or amplifying the natural autonomic response of persons at risk for future criminality. There is very little evidence, therefore, that the drug-crime connection can be attributed to similar patterns of autonomic response for persons predisposed to drug abuse and crime.

Personality

It has been proposed that drug abuse and crime are the natural consequences of addictive (Nakken, 1988) and criminal (Yochelson & Samenow, 1976) personalities. However, research addressing the prospect of an "addiction-prone" personality has found this concept to be largely inadequate from an empirical standpoint (Gendreau & Gendreau, 1970). Hudleby (1986) examined personality factors in a group of 150 early adolescents living in Ontario, Canada, and observed that the personality measures he utilized were generally ineffective in predicting future drug use and delinquency outcomes. There is evidence, however, that drug abuse and crime may be linked by their common association with early antisocial conduct. Hence studies show that childhood conduct problems are convincingly correlated with later substance misuse (Hagnell, Lanke, Rorsman, & Ohman, 1986; Vaillant, 1983) and criminality (Kazdin, 1985; White, Moffitt, Earls, Robins, & Silva, 1990). Personality factors, in the form of early antisocial behavior, might therefore be a potential route of influence through which the drug-crime connection might be studied, explained, and eventually understood.

Though early conduct problems may be responsible for a certain portion of the drug-crime overlap, there are several distinct patterns of precursors important in the formation of a drug or criminal lifestyle. Results from longitudinal studies in Berkeley and Oakland, for instance, indicate that both antisocial and passive-dependent personality features affect a person's future chances of engaging in alcohol- and other drug-related activities. These studies show that persons who exhibit passive-dependent traits during childhood and early adolescence follow a pattern of "late onset" alcohol and tobacco misuse that peaks during middle adulthood, whereas early antisocial traits give rise to a pattern of "early onset" substance misuse that peaks during late adolescence and is accompanied by other forms of acting-out behavior, including crime (Block, 1971). Hence, although early antisocial behavior may prompt some people to engage in both drug abuse and adult criminality, it leaves a major segment of the drug-crime overlap unexplained.

Person Historical-Developmental Conditions and the Drug-Crime Connection

Research has consistently indicated that a diagnosis of antisocial personality is often a robust correlate of alcoholism (Nathan, 1988; Vaillant, 1983) and drug addiction (Egger, Webb, & Reynolds, 1978; Sutker, Moan, Goist, & Allain, 1984) and that early antisocial behavior is an effective predictor of future drug (Hagnell et al., 1986) and criminal (White et al., 1990) outcomes. This association occurs even when the diagnostic overlap between alcoholism/drug dependency and antisocial personality is controlled for (Lewis,

Cloninger, & Pais, 1982), although conventional wisdom holds that the drug-crime connection, at least where historical-developmental conditions are concerned, is principally a function of the high rate of substance abuse problems in antisocial populations (Lewis et al., 1983). In further support of a noninteractive relationship between substance abuse and a diagnosis of antisocial personality, Stabenau (1986) cites research conducted on patients at the University of Connecticut Health Sciences Center that highlights two etiologic pathways for alcohol abuse: One is associated with a positive family history of alcoholism, and the other is associated with the subject's own antisocial behavior.

Utilizing Cloninger's (1987) two-group typology for alcoholism and data gathered on a large group of Swedish adoptees, Cloninger, Bohman, and Sigvardsson (1981) determined that Type I (milieu-limited) alcohol abuse was more prominent in male subjects with alcoholism in at least one adoptive and one biological parent. Conversely, Type II (male-limited) alcohol abuse failed to correspond with the alcohol abuse status of the adoptive home but was observed in male adoptees whose biological fathers had been treated for alcoholism and serious criminality during adolescence or early adulthood. There was a threefold increase in alcohol abuse in female adoptees born to Type I alcoholic fathers, but no increase in either alcohol abuse or criminality for female adoptees born to Type II alcoholic fathers. These findings, coupled with the fact that antisocial behavior appears to be a more powerful correlate of alcoholism for females than for males (Lewis & Bucholz, 1991), suggest that biological and other person historical-developmental conditions do a poor job of explaining the drug-crime overlap.

Situation Variables

Situational historical-developmental conditions are features of a person's external environment (e.g., cultural teachings, social class, family environment, peer relations) that influence the probability of a future drug or criminal outcome.

Cross-Cultural Effects

The reader should know that alcoholism, drug abuse, and crime are not uniformly distributed across societies and cultures; indeed, they vary widely even for persons living within a given general geographic area. In many cases, cross-national differences in substance abuse and crime have been ascribed to differences in cultural attitudes. Strong prohibitions against adolescent alcohol use in Ireland, for instance, correspond with a reduced rate of social and abusive drinking on the part of Irish youth (Christiansen & Teahan, 1987), and cultural attitudes toward female alcohol use vary in accordance with the amount of alcohol consumed by Japanese women living in Japan, Hawaii, and California (Kitano, Chi, Rhee, Law, & Lubben, 1992). Cultural teachings may also exert profound influence over a person's comportment while intoxicated (Cinquemani, 1975). Some researchers, however, such as de Lint (1976), argue that cultural attitudes and values are overrated as explanations of cross-national variations in drug use and abuse, and that factors such as urbanization and availability are of equal value in understanding culture-based differences.

Variations in urbanization and cultural attitudes or informal social controls have also been used to explain cross-national discrepancies in crime. This implies a possible avenue of overlap in the cross-national correlates of drug abuse and crime. One might even be tempted to conclude that cross-cultural effects account for a significant portion of the drug-crime connection on the strength of the presumption that the cross-national correlates of drug abuse and crime are similar, if not identical. Empirical support for a cross-national explanation of the drug-crime connection, however, tends to be rather weak, given that some countries, such as France, Italy, and Switzerland, suffer high rates of alcohol abuse but enjoy below-average rates of crime, in comparison with the United States, which leads the industrialized world in most crime categories but experiences only a moderate degree of alcohol abuse. Consequently, there is little support for the argument that cross-cultural attitudes or practices clarify the nature of the drug-crime connection.

Poverty and Social Class

Few people would take issue with the inference that impoverished urban areas suffer much higher rates of crime and drug abuse than most suburban middle-class areas. Controversy continues to rage, however, on how these findings should be interpreted. A longitudinal investigation by Brunswick (1988) and a cross-sectional study by Clayton and Voss (1981) reveal that drug abuse is rampant in areas where it is most available, namely, in the run-down slum sections of major cities. Likewise, criminologists have determined that crime is concentrated in impoverished urban precincts (Loftin, McDowall, & Boudouris, 1989). The significance and causal nature of this relationship, however, have been hotly contested (Tittle, Villemez, & Smith, 1978). There is even speculation that crime may, in some cases, cause poverty by lowering property values, ravaging informal social control networks, and reducing opportunities for legitimate employment (Stewart, 1986).

Even if social class and poverty do play major roles in the development of drug abuse and crime, there is nothing to indicate that these variables are responsible for the drug-crime connection. This is because the effects of social class and poverty on drug abuse and crime occur through social learning. People observe and imitate the behavior of those with whom they come into contact, whether family, friends, or neighbors. Additional factors, such as the perceived status of the individual being observed and the anticipated reward for the behavior being displayed, determine whether the modeled behavior is enacted (Bandura, 1977). Hence a child who observes alcohol abuse in someone he or she admires or who holds to the expectancy that selling drugs will open up opportunities that would otherwise be unavailable will tend to perform these behaviors. The results of research conducted on poverty and social class therefore indicate one possible interpretation of the drug-crime connection: Drugs and crime are linked by the action of a third variable, that variable being the opportunity to learn specific behaviors from persons living in one's immediate environment.

Family Environment

The family is usually the first social unit with which the child interacts. As a consequence, a person's early lessons in life are often learned in interaction with parents and siblings, the product of which sets the stage for future attitudinal and behavioral development. The family would therefore seem to be capable of affecting future drug use behavior through the intermediary actions of modeling (Ahmed, Bush, Davidson, & Ionnotti, 1984), separation (Friedman, Pomerance, Sanders, Santo, & Utada, 1980), parent-child bonding (Chein, Gerard, Lee, & Rosenfeld, 1964), and disciplinary style (Emmelkamp & Heeres, 1988). Likewise, research on the familial correlates of criminal behavior denote that modeling (McCord, 1988), family conflict (Van Voorhis, Cullen, Mathers, & Garner, 1988), attachment style (Walters & White, 1990), and parenting issues (Wells & Rankin, 1988) are also important precipitants of criminal behavior. Hence there would appear to be commonality in the familial correlates of drug abuse and crime.

Research has convincingly demonstrated that the families of substance abusers and criminals are often the recipients of minimal amounts of social support and are beset with frequent interpersonal conflict. A team of investigators under the direction of Ronald Simons, in fact, found evidence of a robust association between parental rejection and offspring deviance in the form of substance abuse (Simons, Conger, & Whitbeck, 1988; Simons & Robertson, 1989) and delinquency (Simons, Robertson, & Downs, 1989). Simons and his colleagues speculate that parental rejection exerts both direct and indirect effects (by damaging children's self-esteem and encouraging their affiliation with deviant peers) on future aggression and drug use outcomes (Simons et al., 1988). Though family functioning may forge a gateway through which the drug-crime connection can be more precisely defined, the possibility that the similarity in correlate patterns for drug abuse and crime is due to the action of a third variable (e.g., modeling, disciplinary practice) cannot be ruled out on the basis of currently available information. Hence family variables do not necessarily speak to the nature and development of the drug-crime connection.

Peer Relations

It is commonly believed that the single most powerful predictor of adolescent drug use is the degree to which the juvenile associates or "hangs out" with drug-using peers (Kandel & Adler, 1982; Kaplan, Martin, & Robbins, 1984). A relationship has also been observed between peer relations and delinquent behavior (Fagan & Wexler, 1987; Patterson & Dishion, 1985). The results of a study by Giordano, Cernkovich, and Pugh (1986), however, call into question traditional interpretations of the peer-deviance relationship. Contrary to the "cold and brittle" image of delinquent relationships espoused by social control theorists, delinquents in the Giordano et al. study were more likely than nondelinquent youth to share intimacies with one another. Further, inimical to the predictions of the subcultural model, which holds to an "intimate fraternity" interpretation of the delinquency-peer relationship, delinquents reported a higher degree of conflict with other delinquents, their friends, than did nondelinquents. There was also confirmation of a reciprocal interaction effect for delinquent associations whereby individual subjects had as much influence on the functioning of a delinquent group as the delinquent group had on individual subjects.

More than 50 years ago, Edwin Sutherland (1939) argued that a person exposed to an excess of definitions favorable to violation of the law and an absence of definitions unfavorable to violation of the law would be prone to engage in law-violating behavior (see Sutherland & Cressey, 1978); this supposition continues to find support in the research literature on drug abuse and delinquency (see Matsueda, 1988; Orcutt, 1987; Tittle, Burke, & Jackson, 1986). Recent evidence, however, suggests that the actions of deviant peers are actually more influential than their attitudes in promoting future delinquent behavior (Warr & Stafford, 1991). This corroborates research on the role of peer modeling in drug use initiation (Johnson, Marcos, & Bahr, 1987) and suggests that Sutherland's ideas need to be better integrated with social learning theory (see Akers, 1985). There is also proof that although the conduct of friends is a strong predictor of both juvenile drug use and delinquency, there is no clear crossover relationship between these two forms of deviance (White, Johnson, & Garrison, 1985). This review suggests that although drug abuse and crime are strongly influenced by peer factors, there is no material evidence that this situation-based historical-developmental condition effectively clarifies the nature of the drug-crime connection.

Situation Historical-Developmental Conditions and the Drug-Crime Connection

It would seem self-evident not only that situational variables contribute to the formation of drug-seeking behavior and crime, but that drug abuse and law-violating conduct share many of the same situational correlates. Aside from a direct causative model of drug-crime interrelationship (i.e., drugs causing crime or crime causing drug abuse), this correlational overlap can be explained in one of two ways. One possible explanation of drug-crime concordance in situation-based historical-developmental conditions is that drug abuse and crime exist as interdependent features of a wider deviant subculture or syndrome (see Donovan & Jessor, 1985; Hirschi, 1969). A second plausible explanation for the drug-crime correlation observed with situation-based historical-developmental conditions holds that drugs and crime are causally unconnected and linked only by their common association to one or more sociological conditions (see Akers, 1984).

The majority of studies conducted to date tend to support the shared influence model over the general deviance theorem of drug-crime interrelationships (Fagan et al., 1990; White et al., 1985). Probing this issue with longitudinal data, Wayne Osgood and his colleagues discovered that the general deviance model accounted for only a small portion of the variance shared by five forms of deviant behavior (heavy alcohol use, marijuana use, other illicit drug use, dangerous driving, significant criminal behavior), the only direct (causative) effect being the influence of early marijuana use on later involvement with other illicit substances (Osgood, Johnston, O'Malley, & Bachman, 1988). Likewise, Rowe and Gulley (1992) witnessed a sibling effect for drug use and delinquency that implicated mutual friendships and common consensual processes in the genesis of deviant behavior. As it would seem that the shared influence model of drug-crime intercorrelations is more viable than the deviant subculture explanation, the task before us is to identify the "common" or "linking" variables that constitute this shared influence.

One such linking variable might conceivably be the action of a distinct and reliable set of consensually held values, because research has shown that a sense of "cultural responsibility" may impede drug abuse and crime, but not necessarily through a common mechanism. These values and prescriptions should be clear, consistent, and specific rather than nebulous, arbitrary, and general, for as has been demonstrated in studies conducted in the field of social psychology, values are more readily accepted if they are presented free of reservation and contradiction (Rokeach & Ball-Rokeach, 1989). The clarity branch of value adoption shows that crime (Adler, 1983) and drug abuse (Larson & Abu-Laban, 1968) are more common in cultures and societies that are equivocal in their prescriptions for appropriate behavior. The role of consistency in value development is substantiated by research indicating higher rates of crime and drug abuse in cultures that are unclear in defining socially acceptable behavior (Archer & Gartner, 1984). Finally, the specificity component is corroborated by Cinquemani (1975) in his research on the Los Pastores Indians of Central Mexico, who associate violence with drinking except under highly circumscribed conditions (i.e., religious ceremonies) and whose behavior while intoxicated clearly conforms to these cultural prescriptions.

A second possible linking variable with respect to the drug-crime connection is the modeling of deviant behavior. It is well known that young children seek out and identify role models to emulate. When these role models are absent from the home, the child may look elsewhere for personal guidance (Rohrer & Edmonson, 1960). This, in fact, may be the primary path through which peers influence future drug and criminal outcomes. As I have noted throughout this chapter, drug use and delinquency demonstrate clear signs of overlap, especially during adolescence, when peer influence is strong (Lewis et al., 1982). It may very well be that the modeling function of peer relations encourages teenagers to experiment with drugs and crime. Simons, Conger, and Whitbeck (1988), among others, contend that drugs and crime are correlated largely because they have a common heritage in peer relations geared toward the glorification of immediate goals and devaluation of future-oriented concerns. Modeling and peer influence may be instrumental not only in initiating drug use and criminality, but in maintaining these behaviors as well. However, it appears likely that other influences (e.g., career aspirations, the desire to justify one's actions) eclipse modeling and peer influences in significance as the individual moves into the latter stages of a drug or criminal lifestyle.

Most criminals and drug abusers were raised by law-abiding citizens who, although they may have used alcohol or prescription drugs, were not criminal offenders or drug addicts themselves. In other words, although some criminals, and a slightly larger percentage of drug abusers, model the problematic behavior of their parents, many others do not. Weak internalization of parental values, practices, and prohibitions may therefore play an even more salient role in the development of a drug or criminal lifestyle than the modeling of parental behavior. Lifestyle theory maintains that internalization derives from an interaction of variables orbiting around the child, his or her parents, and their mutual relationship. As such, a person's vulnerability to future drug or criminal outcomes is viewed to be a function of a complex interplay of variables involving a high-risk child and parents who feel overwhelmed by the stress of raising a child and dealing with the problems of everyday living. It is the Person × Situation interaction, not individual person or situation variables, therefore, that contributes most forcefully to future behavioral outcomes, whether the focus of our attention is on drug abuse, crime, or more constructive forms of behavior.

Person × Situation Interaction Variables

Lifestyle theory maintains that conditions affect behavior through a constellation of individual person and situation variables. The interactive relationships that form between sundry person and situation variables, however, are believed to exert potent influences over behavior. Lifestyle theory conceptualizes these Person × Situation interactions as occurring in three primary domains of human experience relative to the early life tasks that put an individual at increased or decreased risk for future drug or criminal outcomes. Within the social domain of human experience, Person × Situation interactions congeal around the early life task of attachment, whereas in the physical domain these interactions center on the early life task of stimulus modulation. Interactions taking place in the psychological domain, on the other hand, give rise to the self-image life task.

Attachment

Psychologists and psychiatrists hold that early family relationships set the tone for later interpersonal attitudes and associations. One of the foremost experts on parent-child attachment, Mary Salter Ainsworth (1979), has constructed a system of classification that divides mother-infant attachment into three primary categories: secure, avoidant, and anxious/ambivalent. The person (child) variables that allegedly contribute to future attachment problems include a difficult temperament (Goldsmith & Campos, 1982), early constitutional anomalies (Connell, 1976), infant fearfulness (Goldsmith, Bradshaw, & Rieser-Danner, 1986), low birth weight (Bell, 1979), and persistent crying (Thompson, 1986). Maternal warmth (Bates, Maslin, & Frankel, 1985), acceptance (Main, Tomasini, & Tolan, 1979), and responsiveness (Blehar, Lieberman, & Ainsworth, 1977), on the other hand, contribute to attachment outcomes from the standpoint of being important situational (caregiver) influences. The interaction of these various person and situation variables, however, determines more concisely how the attachment life task plays out.

The results of research on social bonding and drug use (Marcos, Bahr, & Johnson, 1986) imply that ineffective bonding or attachment may be important in the early stages of a drug lifestyle. Ainsworth's (1979) model, however, considers two different styles of inferior bonding—avoidant and anxious/ambivalent—and lifestyle theory contends that people who have resolved this early life task by becoming anxious or ambivalent about intimate relations are at increased risk for future drug involvement. Having been exposed to early life experiences that encourage dependency and discourage self-sufficiency, the anxious/ambivalent subject is drawn to other people as a source of protection and guidance. In fact, the use of mind-altering substances can be viewed as a further extension of this individual's dependency-seeking interests. In contrast, persons forming an avoidant or insecure style of attachment are viewed from the perspective of lifestyle theory as being at increased risk for future criminality. Findings from several different sources provide preliminary support for this supposition (Cadoret & Cain, 1980; Walters & White, 1990). It is speculated that an avoidant style of attachment puts a person at increased risk for predatory criminal conduct by interfering with the development of his or her ability to empathize with and relate to others.

Stimulus Modulation

Stimulus modulation, with roots extending back to the interactive relationship that forms between individual person and situation variables in the physical domain of human experience, provides an index of how the subject perceives, interprets, and organizes sensory information in an effort to achieve an optimal level of physiological arousal. Research suggests that high sensation seeking is meaningfully correlated with drug use/abuse (Andrucci, Archer, Pancoast, & Gordon, 1989) and delinquency (Simo & Perez, 1991) and speaks to the possibility of an interaction of prenatal, perinatal, and postnatal factors. Of the person variables hypothesized to be instrumental in the development of stimulation-seeking tendencies, genetics, neurological factors, and gender are of prime etiologic significance. Parental discipline and environmental stimulation, on the other hand, appear to be the situational influences of greatest potential consequence in determining a person's approach to the stimulation-seeking life task.

Lifestyle theory holds that physical stimulation-seeking tendencies place a subject at escalated risk for future criminal involvement, and a combination of both physical and mental stimulation-seeking interests substantially increase a person's risk for future drug abuse outcomes. This should not be taken to mean that sensation seeking is necessarily bad or that such tendencies should be discouraged in children. In point of fact, many important scientific discoveries and physical feats owe their accomplishment to the high mental and/or physical energy of their authors (Farley, 1986). The culprit is not high sensation interests, but high sensation seeking in combination with less-than-desirable environmental experiences and conditions. Therefore, a proper understanding of the role of stimulation seeking or any of the early life tasks in future deviance development requires consideration of a complex network of interacting influences directly and indirectly related to the outcome of each early life task.

Self-Image

Developmental psychologists assert that newborn infants are incapable of discriminating between themselves and their external environments (Werner, 1957). Over time, however, children learn to separate themselves from their environments. Self-identity and self-perception, founding features of an evolving self-image, derive from a child's ability to differentiate him- or herself from the wider physical environment. Physical attributes, including body type (Sheldon, 1954) and minor physical anomalies such as wide-set eyes and low-set ears (Mednick & Kandel, 1988), are among the person variables potentially capable of explaining the content of a child's self-image. On the situational side of the equation, parental communication and abuse (Dishion, Stouthamer-Loeber, & Patterson, 1984) as well as peer relations (Panella, Cooper, & Henggeler, 1982) help shape the outcome of the self-image life task. Resolution of the self-image life task modifies the person's risk for future drug or criminal involvement by affecting his or her evolving sense of personal identity.

A consummate understanding of the relationship between self-image and future drug and criminal outcomes would appear to require additional study and more eloquent theoretical clarification, perhaps with the aid of object relations theory. One of the major theorists in the object relations field, Otto Kernberg (1972), asserts that there are four stages in the development of stable object relations. Self-perceptions that are split off into "good-me" and "bad-me" components but are not effectively integrated because of problems occurring during the third stage of object relations development may serve as the groundwork for a self-image that lends itself to future criminal involvement. If accurate, this may account for the observation of both high and low self-esteem in the reports and behavior of delinquents (Rosenberg, Schooler, & Schoenbach, 1989). Problems occurring during the fourth stage of Kernberg's model lead to better-integrated, but nonetheless negative, self-perceptions because the content of the parental messages is largely pernicious. It is speculated that such difficulties may place a person at increased risk for future substance abuse problems without appreciably affecting his or her risk of becoming initially involved in criminal activity.

Interactive Historical-Developmental Conditions and the Drug-Crime Connection

Variables contributing to Person × Situation interactions occurring in each of the three primary domains of human experience—social, physical, and psychological—and hypothesized outcomes for drug and criminal development with respect to these three domains are outlined in Table 2.1. It should be noted, however, that certain effects or variables may play more focal roles in the formation of a drug lifestyle than in the genesis of a criminal lifestyle, and vice versa. Hence gender may be a more powerful risk factor for criminality than for drug abuse with respect to interactions taking place in the physical domain (stimulus modulation) of human experience, and infant fearfulness may be more critical in defining a person's risk for drug involvement than in defining risk of serious criminality as part of an interacting web of variables that give rise to the attachment life task. These individual components of Person × Situation interaction and the hypothesized outcomes thought to put an individual at increased risk for future drug or criminal involvement obviously require additional study and evaluation before than can be seen as anything more than conjectural.

In gauging the value of Person × Situation interactional effects for comprehending the drug-crime connection, once again we come up short. Other than the observation that persons at risk for future drug abuse or criminal difficulties, like all people, are confronted by three early life tasks, there is little in the way of empirical evidence with which to substantiate the theory that the Person × Situation interaction of historical-developmental conditions explains the drug-crime connection. This may reflect the hypothetical nature of the system as it currently stands, though it is difficult to escape the conclusion that historical-developmental conditions have little to contribute to the formation of a comprehensive understanding of the drug-crime overlap. As is the case with research on person and situation historical-developmental conditions, there is no compelling evidence that interactive historical-developmental conditions provide us with much insight into the nature, purpose, or connotations of drug-crime overlap. For this reason we turn our attention to current-contextual conditions.

Current-Contextual Conditions

Person Variables

There are sufficient data to suggest that negative affect, in the form of anger, frustration, and depression, is a common precipitant of relapse in substance abuse (Bradley, Phillips, Green, & Gossop,

TABLE 2.1 Overview of the Three Early Life Tasks of Lifestyle Theory

	Life Tasks		
	Attachment	*Stimulus Modulation*	*Self-Image*
Interactive components			
person variables	genetics; temperament	genetics; neurologics; gender	physique; physical attractiveness; physical anomalies; hemispheric organization
situation variables	maternal acceptance and warmth	parental discipline; environmental stimulation	parental communication; peer relations
Outcomes			
drug lifestyle	anxious/ ambivalent	mental and physical sensation seeking	poor self-esteem; low self-confidence
criminal lifestyle	avoidant	physical sensation seeking	unstable self-identity; power-oriented interests

1989) and criminal (Cusson & Pinsonneault, 1986) populations. Although the results of studies addressing emotional disorder as a historical-developmental condition tend to be equivocal (O'Connor, Berry, Morrison, & Brown, 1992), there is preliminary evidence that drug use may serve a self-medicating function in some situations. Thus Newcomb and Bentler (1988) noted that alcohol successfully alleviated depression in a group of adolescents, and Woody, O'Brien, and Rickels (1975) observed a substantial reduction in both depressive symptomatology and subsequent opiate use in heroin addicts treated with antidepressant medication. There may very well be an interactive relationship between drug use and current-contextual emotional issues in which emotional problems inspire a drug use episode, the consequences of which precipitate stress and negative affect and the use of more drugs. Negative affect would appear to have a comparable effect on relapse in criminal offenders (Pithers, Marques, Gibat, & Marlatt, 1983).

As the relationship between emotional issues and drug abuse/ crime implies, current-contextual conditions may do a better job of explaining the drug-crime connection than do historical-development conditions. It would seem apparent, then, that emotional issues and problems form an interlocking system of factors that (a) artificially bond drug use with crime through the action of some third variable or (b) constitute a true system of drug-crime affiliation. With reference to the second hypothesis, it is imaginable that drug use may interfere with an individual's judgment and inhibitions, which, in turn, expands that person's probability of engaging in a criminal act. It is equally plausible that someone who experiences guilt, anxiety, or discomfort following the commission of a particular criminal act may choose to imbibe drugs as a means of quieting these troublesome feelings. This contrasts sharply with the largely negative results achieved by the historical-developmental correlates of drug abuse and crime, suggesting that future research on the drug-crime connection might prove more useful if the focus is shifted to current-contextual conditions.

Situation Variables

A variety of situation-based current-contextual conditions may affect the probability of a concurrent drug or criminal event. Environmental cues, interpersonal conflict, social influence, and drug availability are among the situation variables potentially capable of stimulating a drug use episode by eliciting craving, provoking frustration, or producing a general sense of hopelessness in someone who states that he or she wants to stop using drugs (Bradley et al., 1989). Likewise, criminal associations (West & Farrington, 1973) and increased opportunities for crime (Cullen, Larson, & Mathers, 1985) are known to enhance the probability of specific criminal events. Cohen and Felson's (1979) routine-activities approach holds that three key elements must be present before a predatory criminal act can occur: a motivated offender, a suitable target, and the absence of capable guardians against crime. Research shows that this model is of value in explaining the situational correlates of homicide. For instance, Richard Felson and his colleagues have witnessed an increased probability of homicide in situations where the victim was intoxicated, in possession of a weapon, or physically aggressive during the assault (Felson & Steadman, 1983), or where bystanders served as instigators rather than as mediators (Felson, Ribner, & Siegel, 1984).

Charles Faupel (1985) investigated the influence of situation-based current-contextual conditions on the drug-crime connection by cross-tabulating dichotomized measures of drug availability with life structure (regular occurring patterns of occupational, domestic, recreational, and criminal activity). High availability of or access to drugs paired with high life structure falls within the purview of the stabilized addict role, whereas low availability coupled with high life structure is diagnostic of the occasional user role. High availability and low life structure define the freewheeling addict role, and low availability and low life structure characterize the street junkie role. Research findings imply that heroin addicts may be at greatest risk for arrest during the street junkie phase because they are more apt to engage in impulsive or high-risk crimes than when drug availability or life structure is high (Faupel, 1987). Faupel and Klockars (1987) speculate that there is little crossover between drug abuse and crime during the occasional user phase, a directional relationship in which crime serves as the putative causal agent during the stabilized addict and freewheeling addict phases, and a directional relationship in which drug addiction serves as the causal agent during the street junkie phase. This provides yet another example of how current-contextual conditions may help clarify the nature of the drug-crime connection.

Person × Situation Interaction

From the perspective of lifestyle theory, learning stems from an ongoing series of Person × Situation interactions. I will discuss the decision-making process that characterizes the current-contextual nature of the Person × Situation interaction in Chapter 3; here I will explore briefly only the more general issue of learning.

Research has portrayed a clear and vibrant relationship between learning and drug use (Henningfield & Goldberg, 1983) as well as between learning and crime (Akers, 1985). Accordingly, deviant behavior, much like any behavior, is learned through basic schedules of reinforcement, stimulus-response associations, and the modeling of other people's conduct. There is some indication, however, that persons at risk for criminal behavior display idiosyncratic or anomalous styles of learning in which they condition poorly to punishment (Hare, 1978), are underresponsive to social reinforcement (Sarbin, Allen, & Rutherford, 1965), and have trouble delaying gratification (Black & Gregson, 1973). It is unclear at this point whether persons at risk for future drug-seeking behavior possess these same idiosyncrasies, but it has been suggested that a lack of persistence may elevate a person's risk for future alcohol-related difficulties (Cynn, 1992). As this brief review suggests, current-contextual conditions appear to shed greater light on the drug-crime connection than do historical-developmental conditions.

Conclusion

The results of this review indicate that historical-developmental conditions may not be particularly efficacious for clarifying the nature of the drug-crime relationship. The majority of such variables either depict little drug-crime overlap (heredity, autonomic response, sociocultural factors) or portray this overlap as being the consequence of some third variable (poverty, family environment, peer relations). One might infer from this, as have Fagan and his colleagues (1990), that drug abuse and crime are essentially independent phenomena linked only by a comparable age progression and parallel sets of correlates. This conclusion may be a bit premature, however, in light of the fact that research investigating the relevance of current-contextual conditions to the drug-crime nexus shows that such conditions may account for a certain portion of the overlap found to exist between drugs and crime. This may also explain why traditional research in the substance abuse and criminology fields, which is primarily concerned with the study of historical-developmental conditions, has had trouble unraveling the drug-crime conundrum.

I would urge those who would conclude that there is no meaningful connection between drug abuse and crime to consider the possibility that even if historical-developmental conditions do not elucidate the drug-crime connection, they may still have value in demarcating the parameters of this elusive affiliation. Crossing autonomic response with socioeconomic status and family management style, for instance, could potentially delineate the boundaries of the drug-crime relationship in that crime may be primary (and drug use coincidental) in low-autonomic-responding subjects raised in middle-class home environments but secondary to drug use in high-autonomic-responding subjects raised in working-class home environments. Clearly, additional research is required before these proposed connections can be granted any degree of scientific credence. In the meantime, we would be well advised to consider other avenues of explanation in our effort to arrive at a complete understanding of the drug-crime connection. To this end, in succeeding chapters I present an examination of the choices, cognitions, and change strategies that are the components of drug and criminal lifestyles.

3. Choice

The universe as seen through the eyes of Sir Isaac Newton left little room for uncertainty or chance. Hence when Newton's deterministic philosophy was adopted by scholars in fields such as psychology and sociology, the prospect of choice was all but eliminated from the list of factors considered potential causes of human behavior. In their single-minded pursuit of evidence in support of Newton's mechanistic view of the world, however, these scientists severely restricted the scope and explanatory power of their theories. Take, for instance, the fact that sole genetic or environmental determination of a behavior precludes change except under conditions in which the genetics or the environment changes. Research, however, suggests that change is possible even in situations where the "precipitating" conditions are not addressed. Explaining the fact that severe alcohol abuse periodically abates without benefit of treatment (Cahalan & Cisin, 1976) or that hardened delinquents regularly profit from enrollment in behavioral skills training programs (Gendreau & Ross, 1987) creates problems for a purely deterministic science. We might therefore want to consider the possibility that choice and decision making have effects on drug use and criminal outcomes.

The authority that choice would appear to have over drug-seeking behavior is chronicled by studies showing that although peers encourage drug experimentation, curiosity may be an even more powerful determinant of initial drug use (Bennett, 1986; Hser, Anglin, & McGlothlin, 1987). In fact, a common theme voiced by opiate abusers attempting to explain their initial use of drugs is their desire to be part of the "drug scene" (Bennett, 1986). Research further suggests that choice may be important in maintaining drug use during the middle stages of the addiction process (Bennett & Wright, 1985). The effect of choice on criminal behavior is also well documented. Having studied data from the New Youth Cohort of the National Longitudinal Survey, Phillips and Votey (1987) surmise that the majority of people who experiment with crime revert to crime-free behavior because of the deterrent effect of apprehension and the availability of alternate, legitimate sources of income. In this chapter I present an examination of the founding tenets of rational choice theory and the deterrent value of legal sanctions. Finding both areas of description lacking, I then move into a discussion of alternative conceptualizations of the decision-making process, and follow this up with a review of the lifestyle model of choice behavior.

Rational Choice Theory

The model that perhaps places the greatest emphasis on choice as an explanation for drug use and crime is the economic or rational choice perspective. Proponents of the rational choice perspective assert that people indulge in drug use and crime because they perceive the benefits of engaging in these behaviors to outweigh the benefits of engaging in alternative courses of action (Becker, 1968). It is assumed, then, that the individual conducts an exhaustive review of the relevant variables, weighing the advantages and disadvantages of each, after which he or she arrives at a rational decision. According to rational choice theory, people seek solutions that possess a high degree of anticipated utility (high benefit, low cost) and avoid solutions that embody low perceived benefit and high perceived cost. The underlying premise of this approach is that a person rationally weighs the options available to him or her at any particular point in time and then goes about selecting the optimal solution.

The rational choice or utilitarian perspective takes into account the decision-making processes of the individual as well as the availability and distribution of economic resources in the environment. Rational choice theorists consequently postulate that crime, drug abuse, and unemployment are correlated because there are fewer legitimate employment opportunities available during harsh economic times. Studies probing this issue have been unable to provide a definitive answer to the question of the overlap between economic deprivation and deviance, although the bulk of evidence suggests the presence of a modest relationship between crime and economic factors (see Orsagh & Witte, 1981) and a mild to moderate association between drug abuse and various economic indicators (see Brunswick, 1988). A further criticism of rational choice theory is that although the results of aggregate-level studies may be consistent with the basic tenets of the economic approach (Brier & Fienberg, 1980; Cook, 1980), individual-level studies are much less supportive of the model's underlying assumptions (Piliavin, Gartner, Thornton, & Matsueda, 1986).

Rational choice theory has also been cited for failure to distinguish between objective and subjective estimates of reward and punishment. The mechanistic model proposed by rational choice investigators largely ignores the salient contributions made by perception to the human decision-making process, because it assumes that the objective and subjective features of environmental contingencies are comparable, if not identical. However, research shows this assumption to be erroneous in the sense that the subjective or perceptual features of a contingency are generally superior to the objective features in predicting future decision-making behavior (Waldo & Chiricos, 1972). A reasonable conclusion might therefore be that although choice could very well be important in the initiation and maintenance of drug-seeking and criminal behavior, the manner in which decisions are made is a far cry from the mechanical process proposed by rational choice theory.

The Deterrence Hypothesis

The deterrence hypothesis, which derives from the rational choice model, states that legal sanctions discourage future drug and criminal involvement. Two early proponents of this theoretical perspective, Cesare Becaaria and Jeremy Bentham, were of the opinion that human motivation was a rational, hedonistic (pursuit of pleasure, avoidance of pain), contingency-based process. Gibbs (1975) provides a modern translation of the deterrence hypothesis in which he postulates that the deterrent value of a particular punishment is inversely proportional to the certainty (predictability of consequences), severity (harshness of consequences), and celerity (rapidity of consequences) of that punishment. Deterrence is thought to exert its influence on human behavior by way of an internalization of societal norms, concerns about legal retribution, and a fear of social disapproval (Grasmick & Green, 1980). What follows is a discussion of legal sanctions as impediments to drug use and crime; according to the deterrence hypothesis, legal sanctions should inhibit such activity.

Research has fairly conclusively demonstrated that legal sanctions do not deter or inhibit future illegal drug usage (Meier & Johnson, 1977; Meyers, 1980). Erickson (1976) interviewed a group of first-time offenders in Toronto, Canada, who were awaiting hearings for cannabis possession, and determined that 84% planned to continue using marijuana despite the legal trouble they were facing. Contrary to the predictions of deterrence theory, more severe sanctions and a higher perceived certainty of punishment seemed to encourage, rather than deter, stated plans for future cannabis use in this group of subjects. Further, if legal sanctions deter future drug involvement, then drug use should increase when legal sanctions are loosened or suspended. However, in countries where legal restrictions on drug use have been relaxed or removed, a decrease, rather than the expected increase, in drug use activity has been observed (Ministry of Welfare, Health, and Cultural Affairs, 1985). Furthermore, relaxation of the marijuana laws in 11 U.S. states during the mid-1970s failed to give rise to a noticeable escalation in the rate of marijuana use in these states and jurisdictions (Johnston, Bachman, & O'Malley, 1981).

Studies assessing the deterrent value of legal sanctions for the purposes of reducing criminal behavior are no more encouraging than research on legal sanctions and drug use. The general consensus of cross-sectional studies indicates that although sanction certainty may influence an individual's future probability of engaging in myriad criminal activities, the perceived severity of sanctions has little effect on future criminal outcomes (Paternoster, 1987; Waldo & Chiricos, 1972). The results of longitudinal investigations furnish only modest support for sanction certainty and no support for sanction severity as deterrents to future criminal and delinquent behavior (Bishop, 1984; Paternoster & Iovanni, 1986; Piliavin et al., 1986). In a longitudinal panel study with two follow-up evaluations conducted one year apart, Paternoster (1989) determined that perceived severity had no discernible effect on subjects' decisions to offend or desist from offending, perceived certainty had a modest to moderate effect on subjects' decisions to smoke marijuana and engage in vandalism, and extralegal factors (moral values, opportunity, informal social control) outperformed both perceived severity and perceived certainty in forecasting future criminal outcomes.

Like the rational choice perspective, the deterrence hypothesis has a great many limitations when applied to human behavior. Research has shown that the severity of punishment is a poor predictor of drug use and crime, and the certainty of punishment is only moderately prognostic of future drug and criminal behavior. Research on the proposed relationship between sanction celerity and future deviance has been too sparse to permit even a preliminary conclusion at this point. In general, however, there is little convincing evidence that legal sanctions discourage drug use or crime. However, this may be a consequence of how rational choice theory and the deterrence hypothesis define the decision-making process. As the reader may recall, economic theories of human behavior contend that people weigh their alternatives and then select optimal solutions or courses of action. It may well be that choice and decision making influence drug use and criminal activity but that legal sanctions do not exert their intended effect because the human decision-making process is more complex, idiosyncratic, and biased than rational choice theorists have hypothesized.

The Imperfect Nature of the Choice Process

The validity of the assumption that the human decision-making process is a rational, efficient, and optimizing enterprise has been brought into serious question by the results of studies on shortcut decision making (Corbin, 1980) and perseverative choice selection (Einhorn & Hogarth, 1978). There is also ample evidence to suggest that serious crime tends to be impulsive and spontaneous rather than rational and profit oriented (Fattah, 1982). The irrationality of the decision-making process leading to drug use has also been discussed at length (Denoff, 1988; Shorkey & Sutton-Smith, 1983). Research further indicates that potential outcomes in a decisional matrix are not given equal weight because subjects frequently lose sight of consequences that are either distant or outside their sphere of control (Ainslie, 1982). These findings point to several possible

routes of influence through which nonrational factors might potentially have an impact on the human decision-making process.

In an effort to address the process of criminal decision making,
John Carroll (1978) manipulated the probability of success (.1, .3,
.8), the likelihood of capture (.05, .15, .4), the amount of money to
be gained if successful ($100, $1,000, $10,000), and the anticipated
penalty if unsuccessful (probation, six months incarceration, two
years incarceration) in a series of crime scenarios and presented them
to groups of criminals and noncriminals. Exposing subjects to 72
different crime opportunities, Carroll determined that both criminals and noncriminals relied almost exclusively on one or two of
these four dimensions in rendering a crime/no crime decision.
Though there were no significant offender/nonoffender differences
in the number of dimensions considered, offenders overestimated
their chances of success, ability to evade capture, and anticipated
payoffs relative to the nonoffender control group. Consistent with
Carroll's conclusions, research has convincingly demonstrated that
criminals, particularly those with extensive histories of criminal
involvement, are more confident in the ultimate success of their
unlawful ventures and less concerned about arrest than are noncriminals or criminals who have committed fewer offenses (Henshel &
Carey, 1975; Waldo & Chiricos, 1972).

From the results of Carroll's study we might conclude that human
choice is more a "psychological" phenomenon, subject to error and
oversimplification, than it is a mechanical process characterized by
utilitarian analysis of life options. This tends to support the formu-
lations of Slovic, Fischoff, and Lichtenstein (1977), who propose an
information-processing model of human decision making whereby the
individual utilizes simple comparisons and partial examinations rather
than an all-inclusive review of alternatives. Similar trends have been
identified in the thinking of burglars (Hough, 1987; D. Walsh,
1986), robbers (Feeney, 1986), shoplifters (Weaver & Carroll,
1985), commercial thieves (Gibbs & Shelly, 1982), and opiate
addicts (Bennett, 1986). This may explain why rational choice
theory and the deterrence hypothesis have accrued only limited
empirical support in studies on drug abuse and crime. Given that
the decision-making process appears to operate in a manner different
from that proposed by economic theories of crime and drug abuse,
it may be helpful to take a look at how criminal offenders and drug
abusers arrive at their crime- and drug-oriented decisions.

Floyd Feeney (1986) examined the decision-making responses of
113 men from Northern California who were charged with robbery

and convicted of either robbery or robbery-related offenses. Of these men, 57% listed "money" as their primary motive for committing robbery. Other expressed motives included anger (6%), boredom (6%), power (6%), and the recovery of money the subjects thought was owed them (5%). Robberies were apparently unplanned in more than half the cases, and in another third only minor planning took place. Comparing groups of experienced and inexperienced shoplifters, Weaver and Carroll (1985) determined that novice or inexperienced shoplifters were deterred by fear, guilt, and the possibility of apprehension, whereas the prospect of arrest, fines, or incarceration rarely entered into the deliberations of experienced shoplifters. In reality, the only factor that consistently impeded experienced shoplifters from capitalizing on criminal opportunities was the presence of strategic difficulties (e.g., size of the item, security devices). Novices were characteristically deterred in the face of even a single strategic roadblock, but experienced shoplifters conceived of strategic difficulties as challenges to be overcome and mastered. As in the earlier study by Carroll (1978), the subjects, regardless of their prior level of experience, normally took only one or two relevant dimensions into account when analyzing the criminal opportunities available to them.

Trevor Bennett (1986) interviewed 135 English heroin addicts in an effort to understand the initiation, continuation, and cessation of opiate use and addiction. In so doing, he ascertained that curiosity and peer acceptance were the two most popular motives for initial heroin involvement, with just 6 of the 135 subjects stating that they felt pressured into using their first opioid. One-third to one-half of the sample, in fact, acknowledged that the decision to use heroin predated their ingestion of opiates by days, weeks, or even months as they actively sought opportunities for drug use. Concerning the onset of addiction, Bennett observed that physical addiction typically did not occur until at least a year after initial heroin use and that periods of abstention and occasional use both preceded and succeeded addiction. Moreover, the decision to continue using heroin was typically based on a desire to experience its pleasant or self-medicating effects rather than on the drive to avoid the pain of withdrawal. Like Feeney's (1986) robbers and Weaver and Carroll's (1985) shoplifters, Bennett's opiate addicts displayed self-determination, intentionality, planning, and deliberation in choosing to use heroin, although, also like the subjects in the Feeney and Weaver and Carroll studies, the decision-making models employed by these individuals were biased, restricted, and shortsighted.

The Lifestyle Model of Choice Behavior

The lifestyle model of choice behavior comprises three basic steps or stages: input, process, and output.

Input Stage

It is well known that the reliability of output derived from a computer is largely dependent on the quality of information entered into it. Much the same could be said of the human decision-making enterprise, although compared to a computer the human brain is a much less efficient processor of information. Accordingly, the decision (output) is a consequence of both the informational input and the manner in which this information has been processed. Four primary forms of informational input are considered below: risk/protective factors, exacerbating/mitigating factors, opportunity, and target selection.

Risk/Protective Factors

Risk factors are historical-developmental conditions that increase the individual's liability for future drug-seeking or criminal behavior; protective factors are variables that decrease the individual's likelihood of engaging in future drug- or crime-oriented activity. Risk/protective factors influence human behavior by narrowing (risk) or expanding (protective) a person's range of options. Therefore, as Donald West and David Farrington (1973) discovered in a survey of data generated by a group of working-class London youth, risk factors augment the probability of subsequent drug-seeking or criminal behavior without actually determining future drug or criminal outcomes. This is reflected in the fact that 13% of the delinquents in their sample (including 17 repeat offenders) failed to satisfy their criteria for high risk as represented by a family history of criminality and the presence of at least two of six adverse sociodemographic conditions. These authors also identified several high-risk youth who chose not to engage in criminal behavior. Though these high-risk individuals were often socially maladjusted in other ways (e.g., substance abuse, social isolation, poor work performance), a handful appeared to have escaped their backgrounds altogether to become happy, successful, contributing members of society.

High-risk paradigms have been proposed in research on both drug abuse (Newcomb, Maddahian, & Bentler, 1986) and crime (Loeber,

1990), and studies suggest that risk and protective factors may operate from opposite ends of the same continuum. Hence high self-esteem may protect an otherwise vulnerable youth from engaging in serious drug-seeking activity (Kandel, 1978), and low self-esteem may place an adolescent at increased risk for future drug involvement (Miller & Jang, 1977). Some high-risk paradigms propose a summative effect for combinations of risk factors. Hence Bry, McKeon, and Pandina (1982) determined that the total number of risk factors was more predictive of alcohol, tobacco, and cannabis use in a group of 973 high school students than any one specific risk factor. Probing the relationship between six risk factors (low social status, large family size, paternal criminality, maternal psychiatric history, severe marital discord, and social service administration involvement) and criminal outcome, Rutter et al. (1975) witnessed a synergistic effect: One risk factor was no more prognostic of crime than a complete absence of risk factors, but the presence of two risk factors produced a fourfold increase in a subject's vulnerability to delinquency, and three or more risk factors elevated the subject's vulnerability to delinquency in further multiplicative fashion.

This brief review suggests that risk factors serve an augmenting function by elevating a subject's liability for future drug or criminal activity, whereas protective factors tend to insulate an already vulnerable individual from additional negative influences, thereby decreasing his or her chances of engaging in future drug or criminal behaviors. Consequently, risk and protective factors assume a prominent position in the lifestyle model of choice behavior. In effect, they establish the parameters of a person's choices by expanding or limiting his or her options. Whether risk factors operate in additive or multiplicative fashion is a question that requires further investigation; that they are important in defining the limits of our decisions, however, can hardly be contested.

Exacerbating/Mitigating Factors

Recall that there are two primary categories of conditions: historical-developmental and current-contextual. Whereas historical-developmental conditions establish an individual's risk for future drug and criminal involvement, current-contextual conditions set the tone for his or her involvement in specific drug or criminal events. Thus the effects of exacerbating/mitigating factors on decision making are more situational and transitory than are risk/protective effects. This does not mean, however, that the same variable cannot serve both a risk/protective and exacerbating/mitigating function. Take, for instance, the relationship between peers and drug abuse. There is ample evidence to suggest that peers play a salient facilitative role in early drug involvement (risk/protective factor), although peers can also exert a contextual effect by either encouraging (exacerbating influence) or discouraging (mitigating influence) the use of drugs in specific situational contexts.

Setting effects also highlight the influence of current-contextual conditions on drug-seeking and criminal-activity-oriented behavior. Drug-related setting effects are responses elicited or influenced by the environment in which drugs are taken. Setting effects have been documented with respect to the use of alcohol (Sher, 1985), marijuana (del Porto & Masur, 1984), and heroin (Zinberg, 1984), although stimulant drugs such as d-amphetamine may be less subject to settings effects relative to alcohol and marijuana (Zacny, Bodker, & de Wit, 1992). Felson and Steadman (1983) have investigated setting effects and crime; after reviewing 159 separate incidents of homicide and assault, they observed a pattern in which a verbal attack was followed by attempts to influence the antagonist and then by physical retaliation when persuasion proved ineffective. In a related study, Felson et al. (1984) determined that third parties wield situational influence over the behavior of persons engaged in arguments or altercations by either encouraging violence (exacerbating influence) or attempting to mediate the dispute (mitigating influence).

Not all current-contextual conditions exert consistent exacerbating or mitigating effects. Take, for instance, the current-contextual condition of money. There is no simple association between a person's current financial situation and his or her inclination toward drug and/or criminal activity. Interviews conducted with offenders such as Feeney's (1986) robbers and Gibbs and Shelly's (1982) commercial thieves reveal that money is not always the chief motivation for acquisition-type crimes. Thus the greed stimulated by a large heist can sometimes lead to an increased, rather than decreased, level of subsequent criminality. Much the same can be said about the relationship between an individual's current financial status and use of drugs, in that during some stages of the drug lifestyle a windfall of money can lead to increased drug use, whereas in another stage or context such newfound fortune will have little impact on the overall level of drug consumption (Faupel, 1987). The exacerbating and mitigating effects of current-contextual conditions on choice behavior constitute a complex, yet potentially enlightening, topic for future research on drug use and crime.

Opportunity

Drug use and crime are infrequent in situations where the opportunity for such behaviors is limited. As Goldman (1981) notes, drug use is a choice that depends on the individual's familiarity with drugs, access to financial resources, and opportunity to purchase, prepare, and use these chemical substances. Three expressions commonly used to describe the behavior of drug addicts, *getting over, hustling,* and *copping,* in fact, illustrate the effect of choice and opportunity on the routine daily activities of someone committed to a drug lifestyle. *Getting over* refers to the fact that even persons addicted to heroin are able to finance their use of drugs and sustain themselves without necessarily resorting to predatory forms of criminal activity (Moore, 1977). The heroin addict is an opportunist who creatively finances his or her drug habit with nonpredatory crime, legitimate employment, contributions from family and friends, and miscellaneous hustling (Goldstein, 1981). *Hustling,* as well, entails choice, calculation, and sensitivity to opportunities (Agar, 1973). Research further indicates that *copping* drugs, a term used to describe the manner in which users pay or barter for drugs, is similar in many ways to the routine activities of the bargain-hunting American consumer (Stephens & Smith, 1976).

The relationship between opportunity and crime is revealed in studies showing that bank robberies multiply in direct proportion to the amount of currency available in banks (Gould, 1969), auto thefts rise in accordance with increases in the number of unprotected automobiles (Wilkins, 1964), and shoplifting rates climb in response to expansion of the absolute number and accessibility of self-service grocery stores (D. P. Walsh, 1978). One interpretation of the positive correlation observed between ambient temperature and violent criminality is that there are more opportunities for human interaction, and thus conflict, during the warmer months of the year (Anderson & Anderson, 1984). In further support of an opportunity-based theory of crime, Felson and Cohen (1977) report that the burglary rate rose and fell between 1950 and 1972 in response to three variables, two of which (percentage of "primary individual" households and mobility of property targets) can be viewed as providing offenders with increased opportunities for crime. Newman's (1972) "defensible space" theory of crime prevention focuses on reducing criminal opportunities by increasing surveillance. Although research on the defensible space theorem is mixed, there is reasonably good support for the notion that opportunity-reducing procedures such as the surveillance techniques advocated by New-man register a discernible preventive effect (MacDonald & Gifford, 1989).

Target Selection

Closely related to the issue of opportunity is the notion of target selection. With regard to drug use, this involves the choice of a substance of abuse; with regard to criminal behavior, it entails identification of a property target or victim. A great deal has been written about the "drug of choice" concept in traditional drug treatment circles. An increasing rate of polydrug abuse (Gawin & Ellinwood, 1988; Washton & Gold, 1986) and studies showing drug of choice to be ineffective for classifying drug users (Newcomb, Fahy, & Skager, 1988; Walters, in press), however, have led some experts to question the drug of choice concept. Most drug users have considerable experience with a wide variety of substances and are more than willing and able to find substitutes if their preferred drugs are unavailable (Zinberg, 1984). Heroin addicts, in fact, have been known to regulate their usage patterns in response to changes in the available supply and subsequent price of heroin. This may entail reducing the amount of heroin consumed, replacing heroin with a less expensive or more procurable substance (such as alcohol), or entering a methadone maintenance program (Silberman, 1978). Studies conducted in both New York City (Waldorf, 1976) and London (Stimson & Oppenheimer, 1982) indicate that many active narcotics addicts successfully abstain from opiates for periods of a week to several months with only minor discomfort. Availability, cost, and preference are among the factors taken into account by these persons who go about the process of deciding whether to use heroin or other drugs.

Criminals also consider a number of factors in their deliberations relative to identifying potential targets. Several of the more commonly studied dimensions include proximity, accessibility, potential yield, and timing. Hough (1987) examined crime survey data on burglaries in England and Wales for the years 1982 and 1984 and discovered that proximity and accessibility were key factors in target selection, although the selection process usually was poorly planned, clumsy, and largely opportunistic. In fact, more than half the attempts ended in failure, providing further corroboration for Carroll's (1978) argument that the decision-making process culminating in a criminal outcome is oversimplified and error filled. The accessibility of a particular target and the absence of capable guardians against crime (Cohen & Felson, 1979) also provide opportunities for crime (Kennedy & Forde, 1990). With respect to proximity and accessibility, it is known that persons are at increased risk for criminal victimization if their lifestyles bring them into close and regular contact with strangers in potentially conflict-promoting situations (Garofalo, 1987). Target selection as well as risk/protective factors, exacerbating/mitigating factors, opportunity, and a host of unspecified input variables set the stage for the next phase of the decision-making sequence: the organization and processing of input information.

Process Stage

The information-processing approach to behavioral decision making maintains that people employ individualized strategies in constructing decisions but that these strategies consist primarily of simple comparisons and partial examinations (Slovic et al., 1977). According to Becker (1968), the economics of human decision making demand that a set of alternatives be generated, a set of outcomes or payoffs be delineated, and the probability of achieving these outcomes or payoffs be calculated. The individual is said to follow a utilitarian approach to decision making whereby the advantages and disadvantages of one course of action are weighed against the advantages and disadvantages of one or more other courses of action. Unfortunately for the decision maker, as well as for rational choice theory, decisions about drug use and crime, as well as most other behaviors, are not normally this efficient. The human decision-making process is, in fact, crude, flawed, and potentially biased. Accordingly, to comprehend this process we must take into account the developmental context, innate fallibility, reinforcement history, and motivational parameters of the decision-making process.

Developmental Context

The decision-making model proposed by lifestyle theory holds that choice takes place within a developmental context. In other words, a newborn infant does not make choices, at least not in the way we normally conceive of choice. However, with neurocognitive development and an expanding array of environmental experience the individual cultivates the ability to engage in informed decision making. Most 18-month-old children have not learned that taking from others is wrong, whereas the average 8-year-old, because of both neurological maturation and environmental experience, is cognizant of the cultural proscription against stealing. The 16-year-old is even more aware that stealing is wrong, and the 25-year-old is more aware yet. With development and maturation come awareness and an unfolding ability to choose from a shifting set of alternatives.

Jean Piaget's (1963) theories of cognitive development have helped shape our understanding of how the human decision-making process works. We know from research conducted in the field of developmental psychology, much of which has been influenced by Piaget, that the human organism moves through several stages of cognitive and moral development. By age 7, the child has shifted from an egocentric view of the world to an understanding of the fundamental laws of nature and cause and effect; by age 11, the individual has progressed to a stage wherein he or she can appreciate and use abstract concepts and formulate hypotheses about the world (Piaget, 1963). As to choices concerning drug use and crime, research has shown that children as young as 5 years can grasp the concept of motive and intentionality (Berndt & Berndt, 1975), and children as young as 6 are known to place greater emphasis on intention (accidental versus purposeful) than on level of damage (large versus small) in assigning moral judgments to behavior. These findings suggest that many children possess the foundational prerequisites of informed decision making by the time they are 5 or 6 years of age.

A question for which there is no simple answer at this time pertains to the age at which a person becomes an informed decision maker. Dalby (1985), arguing that the age of informed consent and criminal responsibility varies because cognitive development varies, visualizes the age of criminal responsibility, similar in many ways to the concept of informed decision making, as a range extending from mid-childhood (age 7) to mid-adolescence (age 14). Though researchers will likely continue to expend energy to pinpoint the age at which informed choice crystallizes, a more productive approach might be to investigate how this process evolves and matures over time. It would seem likely that the early signs of informed decision making surface around age 2, when the child begins to internalize aspects of his or her external environment (Piaget, 1963). This evolving ability to make decisions expands as the child comes into contact with familial and extrafamilial sources of information, the latter of which include peers, the media, and experience with the criminal justice system. The result is that choice behavior develops and the individual's options expand as a consequence of cognitive maturation and an ever-widening sphere of environmental experience.

Fallibility

The human decision-making process will never be able to match the computer in terms of speed, accuracy, and precision, because of the flawed nature of the human decision-making enterprise. Carroll's (1978) work with adults and Cimler and Beach's (1981) work with adolescents conclusively demonstrates that the decision-making models people normally utilize are unsophisticated, inefficient, and subject to errors of both omission and commission. A significant loss of information often accompanies attempts to organize, synthesize, and combine divergent bits of knowledge into a compact conceptual framework for the purposes of synthesis and storage (Reitman, 1974). What this means is that the human decision maker does not always or even usually derive the optimal solution to a problem. In direct contrast to the proficiency of the computer, the human decision maker is fallible, imperfect, and seriously limited in terms of how much information he or she can store, retain, and process. This explains not only why rational choice theory has received less than maximal empirical support, but also why some people choose to engage in behaviors that seem patently self-destructive.

Reinforcement History

We know from learning theory that people tend to engage in those actions for which they have been reinforced in the past and refrain from enacting behaviors for which they have been punished previously. Therefore, not all options or potential solutions are given equal weight in any one situation, owing to the fact that people prefer solutions that have been reinforced in the past even though they may not be optimal in the present situation. Take, for example, the person who has an argument with his or her spouse and views alcohol as the optimal solution to his or her problem based on prior experience (i.e., alcohol has eliminated bad feelings for the individual in similar situations in the past). This short-term solution to the problem of negative affect, however, will likely create many more long-term problems for the individual once he or she recovers from the influence of the alcohol.

A person's time horizon (Wilson & Herrnstein, 1985) is important to the extent that it divulges how he or she evaluates the potential consequences of his or her conduct. Some people consider only the immediate consequences of a particular course of action, whereas others take certain long-range considerations into account.

In fact, one sign of maturity is the ability to delay gratification and work toward long-term satisfaction. Important individual differences have been noted with respect to time horizons in that persons who opt for small immediate rewards tend to be at greater risk for delinquency and other forms of acting-out behavior than are persons who choose delayed, but larger, rewards (Mischel, 1974). Similar to Mischel's work on delay of gratification and delinquency, research studies reveal a connection between expectancies and drug use. Christiansen and Goldman (1983), for instance, observed that alcohol-related expectancies of enhanced social and physical pleasure from drinking predicted higher levels of alcohol consumption in adolescents tested one year later. More recently, Wood, Nagoshi, and Dennis (1992) noted a relationship between positive outcome expectancies, particularly the expectancy that alcohol would exert a disinhibiting effect, and drinking patterns and problems in a sample of 231 alcohol-using college students.

Experiences arising from continued involvement in a drug or criminal lifestyle are also capable of affecting a person's appraisal of specific rewards and punishments. Individuals ensconced in a drug or criminal lifestyle frequently see increasing rewards as a consequence of their involvement in this lifestyle and discount or belittle the rewards to be found in a nondrug or noncriminal lifestyle (Walters, 1992b). In like fashion, the fear of punishment and the significance attached to the negative long-term consequences of drug (Bennett, 1986) or criminal (Feeney, 1986) involvement tend to diminish with a person's experience in one of these lifestyles. To a large extent, finding reinforcement in being "ordinary," as Biernacki (1990) observed in a group of 101 opiate addicts who abandoned their drug habits without benefit of treatment, is a cardinal feature of relapse prevention, whether the focus is on a drug lifestyle or a criminal one. It is imperative to keep in mind, then, that lifestyle theory conceives of human beings as active participants in their own learning environments, interacting with and influencing their surroundings as much as their surroundings influence them.

Validation

Motivation would appear to be indispensable to a science of human behavior. Considering the fact that motives activate and direct behavior, it is difficult to conceive of human behavior in their absence. Secondary organizing motives important in drug-seeking behavior center on three primary themes: enhancement, coping, and social motives (Critchlow, 1986; Leigh, 1989). The first two themes, enhancement and coping, are of prime consideration in the development of a drug lifestyle. Motives for criminal lifestyle involvement, on the other hand, are of four primary types: anger/rebellion, power/control, excitement/pleasure, and greed/laziness (Walters, 1990). It is a fundamental premise of lifestyle theory that offenses committed within the purview of the criminal lifestyle are a function of one or more of these four motives.

The secondary organizing motives for drug and criminal involvement enter into the decision-making matrix through a process referred to by lifestyle theorists as *validation*. Validation affords the drug abuser or criminal offender a psychological rationale for his or her actions. Hence a substance abuser may justify the use of drugs by pointing to the pleasant and intoxicating feelings produced by these substances (enhancement motive) or the facility with which these chemicals alleviate stress and frustration (coping motive). The criminal offender, on the other hand, may validate his or her criminal actions by citing societal injustice (anger/rebellion), referencing a desire to exert control over others (power/control), seeking thrills and immediate gratification (excitement/pleasure), or satisfying the desire to accumulate material wealth with as little work as possible (greed/laziness). Though validation may not always be within the individual's immediate awareness, it is nonetheless a conscious process and something the individual can be made cognizant of with minimal prodding and assistance.

Output Stage

The output stage of the decision-making model consists principally of the decision to engage in a particular behavior or to refrain from engaging in that behavior. Boiled down to its simplest form, output involves the decision to use or not use a particular drug, to commit or not commit a specific criminal act. The output stage may also give rise to the decision to perform one set of behaviors over another, often incompatible, set of behaviors. Hence, if a person remains at home to study for a test, this would preclude that individual's going downtown and hanging out with delinquent peers, at least for the period in which he or she is studying for the test. Additional plans and considerations covered during the output stage include the selection of associates (who the individual will use drugs with; who he or she will choose as a crime partner), settings (where the person will use drugs; where he or she will commit the crime), and precautionary measures (how the person will avoid getting caught by parents, teachers, police, or others).

The output stage defines the behavioral consequences of the input and processing stages. Although the output derives from the two stages that precede it, the third stage cannot be predicted with absolute certainty from knowledge of the first two stages even if one were to identify all manner of input and understand fully how this input has been processed. This is because lifestyle theory is nondeterministic and allows for the appearance of random events and atypical occurrences. Furthermore, the output stage can influence itself through an informational feedback loop (Pearson & Weiner, 1985) whereby the subject considers future decisions in light of the perceived success or failure of past decisions. Although the lifestyle model of human decision making is nondeterministic in nature, adequate understanding of how information is entered into the equation and then processed can go a long way toward explaining why an individual chooses one specific course of action over other available options at any particular point in time.

Conclusion

Echoing the conclusions of Speckart and Anglin (1986), the present discussion suggests that choice plays a vital role in both drug use and criminal activity. The problem with choice lies not in its existence but in the way it has been envisioned. Choice, as a correlate of drug use and crime, has traditionally been construed to be a rational process characterized by an evaluation of alternative solutions and the selection of an "optimal" course of action. The problem with this conceptualization of the choice process is that, as research has convincingly demonstrated, this is not how the human decision-making process operates. Human decision making is limited rather than comprehensive, biased rather than methodical, and driven by motives rather than by logic. Furthermore, it stands to reason that erroneous, biased, motive-based decision making is particularly characteristic of drug abusers and serious criminals.

In contrast to historical-developmental conditions, which, at best, provide potential markers and parameters of the drug-crime relationship, choice appears to speak more directly to issues of drug-crime overlap, because drug and criminal choices are based on the same flawed and error-filled decision-making process. The decision to commit a crime, for instance, leads to follow-up decisions designed to support this behavior, one of which might be to use drugs. Abusable substances can therefore be used prior to the commission of an offense to eliminate fear and other deterrents to criminal action, or after the commission of a successful crime as part of the "victory" celebration. Either way, the circle soon completes itself, as someone previously committed to a criminal lifestyle initially imbibes drugs to further his or her criminal lifestyle but ends up drifting into a drug lifestyle because of the positive reinforcement this lifestyle has to offer. Similar choice-based transitions occur when someone chooses to commit a crime in order to support a drug lifestyle.

4. Cognition

The limits of the human decision-making apparatus have been considered in detail in Chapter 3. Given these limits, it would stand to reason that the thinking patterns a person uses to support and justify choices and decisions regarding drug use and criminal activity are equally flawed. This, in fact, is precisely what has been observed when this issue has been subjected to empirical scrutiny. Albert Ellis (1962), the founder of rational emotive therapy, has cogently argued that emotional and behavioral problems are grounded in flawed thinking. These thinking patterns, which become increasingly automatic with practice, form the foundation of a drug or criminal lifestyle by virtue of their ability to elicit support from others and justify drug- and crime-oriented activities. The power of thought to reinforce a drug or criminal lifestyle is therefore the focal point of discussion in this chapter.

Cognitive Correlates of Drug Abuse and Crime

Irrational thinking and drug use are linked to the extent that characteristics known to place a person at risk for substance abuse, most notably low self-esteem (Daly & Burton, 1983), anxiety (Himle, Thyer, & Papsdorf, 1982), depression (Nelson, 1977), and emotional distress (Smith, Houston, & Zurawski, 1984), are highly correlated with indices of irrational thinking. This does not necessarily mean, however, that drug use and irrational thinking are causally connected. In an effort to unravel the mysteries of the putative relationship between irrational thinking and drug use, Martin Denoff (1988) perused interview data on juveniles enrolled in a private residential drug treatment program. Subsequent data analyses revealed that mother- and father-interactive variables and irrational thinking accounted for 29% and 17% of the variance in a frequency measure of drug abuse, respectively, however, family structure and parental absence were only minimally related to the drug abuse criterion measure. The greatest levels of drug abuse were observed in subjects who viewed their parents' approval as conditional and who engaged in excessive amounts of catastrophizing and approval-seeking self-talk. In a sample of adult male subjects undergoing treatment for alcohol abuse, Rohsenow et al. (1989) determined that irrational beliefs correlated with problem avoidance, the urge to drink, and susceptibility to relapse during a six-month follow-up period.

Because irrational beliefs are often constructed on tenuous foundations of unrealistic and faulty expectations, research on expectancies and drug use (some of which was mentioned briefly in Chapter 3) would appear to have something to contribute to our understanding of the cognitive features of drug use and abuse. It has been shown that children as young as 12 display clear expectancies concerning the effects of consuming alcoholic beverages on behavior even before they have had any direct experience with alcohol (Christiansen, Goldman, & Inn, 1982). Consequently, acculturation may be as influential as personal experience in defining drug expectancies. Other studies suggest that expectancies measured during early adolescence reliably predict drinking patterns and problems at follow-ups one year (Christiansen & Goldman, 1983) and two years (Smith, Roehling, Goldman, & Christiansen, 1987) later. The expectancy that alcohol will facilitate social relationships and eliminate negative affect, an expectancy clearly influenced by both peer and parental factors (Biddle, Bank, & Marlin, 1980), is common to persons who later experience problems with alcohol or other drugs (Brown, Goldman, Inn, & Anderson, 1980). Expectancies are tied in with not only the choice features of drug use but the cognitive features as well and therefore provide a potential link between the choice and cognition branches of lifestyle theory.

Research on the cognitive features of crime and delinquency was given a much-needed boost by Sykes and Matza's (1970) pioneering work on techniques of neutralization. Arguing that delinquents learn to justify and rationalize their behavior by interacting with other law-violating juveniles, Sykes and Matza observed five primary forms of rationalization or neutralization (denial of responsibility, denial of injury, denial of the victim, condemnation of society, and appeals to higher loyalties) in the thinking of youthful offenders. Henderson and Hewstone (1984) interviewed 44 violent offenders and determined that these individuals regularly justified their participation in various intrusive criminal acts by attributing their behavior to external circumstances (situation, behavior of the victim). Rapists frequently neutralize or justify their sexual violence by positioning their victims in the role of contributory influence (Burt, 1983), and child molesters have been known to neutralize feelings of guilt by convincing themselves that the children benefited from the experience (Stermac & Segel, 1989). Utilizing a 16-item self-report measure of delinquency, Guerra (1989) determined that high-delinquency black youth exceeded low-delinquency black youth in minimizing the significance, severity, and ultimate consequences of their deviant behavior. Benson (1985) observed a similar pattern in a sample of adult white-collar criminals.

The Lifestyle Model of
Drug- and Crime-Oriented Thinking

Specific thoughts can be conceptualized as falling along three primary dimensions or continua: rational versus irrational, controlled versus automatic, and self-educating versus self-justifying. These can be arranged in three-dimensional space by positioning them at right angles to one another (see Figure 4.1). Most people's thinking falls along the full length of each dimension, although some of us entertain more rational thoughts, are more deliberate in our thinking, and are more interested in self-advancement than others of us. Those who become involved in negative lifestyles, whether of the drug, crime, or gambling variety, spend an inordinate amount of time in the irrational/automatic/self-justifying quadrant of Figure 4.1.

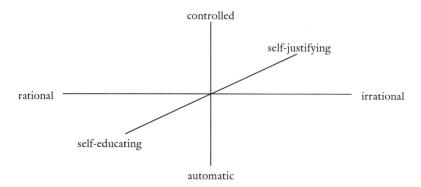

Figure 4.1. Three Dimensions of Human Cognition

This is because the irrational/automatic/self-justifying style of thinking provides a person with the opportunity to continue functioning in a negative lifestyle without having to confront, face, or even acknowledge the full destructive potential of this lifestyle.

The rational versus irrational continuum considers the quality of information upon which a thought is based. A rational thought is one that is free of distortion rather than biased, factual rather than fanciful, and comprehensive rather than limited. As noted in the review of choice and decision making presented in Chapter 3, very few thoughts achieve consummate rationality, although many cognitions do, in fact, approach this ideal. Someone committed to a drug or criminal lifestyle gravitates toward the irrational pole of this continuum, wherein thinking is biased, myopic, and technologically flawed. In considering the rational versus irrational branch of the lifestyle model of cognition it is imperative that rationality not be confused with logic. Where logic is concerned with rules and the application of these rules, rationality provides an index of the accuracy of information entered into a logical equation and upon which decisions are based. Consequently, whereas a small child, an actively psychotic person, or a brain-damaged patient may display disturbed logic, a person consumed with drug or criminal lifestyle activities is simply irrational.

A second dimension on which cognitions differ is the degree to which an individual's thoughts are controlled versus automatic (Strayer & Kramer, 1990). All people, as a consequence of repetition, engage in automatic thinking. This may occur at work (e.g., engaging in a repetitive job task), at home (e.g., eating a meal at a certain time each day), on the road (e.g., stopping at a blinking red light before proceeding), or elsewhere. Although automatic thinking is adaptive to the extent that it permits the rapid execution of routine and repetitive tasks, it becomes problematic when the thoughts being automatized are negative, destructive, or self-defeating. Individuals immersed in a drug or criminal lifestyle repetitively engage in the same destructive activities because their actions are based on negative thoughts that have been rehearsed and repeated so often that they have become automatic. Just as treatment should be directed at teaching the individual to identify and challenge irrational thinking, so too must intervention reinforce the person's capacity for controlled thought.

The third dimension along which thoughts may vary is the degree to which the individual strives for self-education versus self-justification. The self-educating person examines the motivation behind his or her beliefs and seeks to develop a better understanding of his or her world. The self-justifying individual, on the other hand, denies that there is any motivation behind his or her thinking and seeks to protect his or her ideas from the onslaught of reality. As with the other two dimensions, people's thinking falls along the entire spectrum of possibilities, from thoughts that are largely self-educational in nature to thoughts that are heavily laden with self-justifying motives. Someone committed to a drug or criminal lifestyle will engage in an excessive amount of self-justification while avoiding self-education. Expanding one's repertoire of self-educating thoughts requires that one learn to become more receptive to new information and more critical of one's own thoughts and beliefs.

The lifestyle model of drug- and crime-oriented thinking has been noticeably influenced by Yochelson and Samenow's (1976) work on the criminal personality. Based on observations gleaned from several thousand interviews conducted with hardened criminal offenders, these researchers derived a descriptive model of 52 thinking errors. Unfortunately, some of these thinking errors were actually more behavioral or affective in nature, and others were difficult to operationalize or were of dubious clinical value. By starting with five of Yochelson and Samenow's thinking errors—adding, subtracting, and modifying where necessary—and conducting both clinical and research investigations, a colleague and I derived a system of eight thinking styles relevant to both drug abuse and crime: mollification, cutoff, entitlement, power orientation, sentimentality, superoptimism, cognitive indolence, and discontinuity (Walters & White, 1989b). These eight patterns form the groundwork of the third C (cognition) and provide a potential avenue through which the nature of the drug-crime connection might be studied.

Mollification

The cognitive pattern of mollification is conveyed in statements that justify and rationalize drug-seeking and crime-oriented behavior. Mollification is similar in many ways to Sykes and Matza's (1970) neutralization hypothesis, although, in line with Hamlin's (1988) critique of Sykes and Matza's work, mollification is viewed in lifestyle theory as a cognitive strategy that succeeds rather than precedes the behavior it is designed to justify. Of course, mollifications used to justify one activity after the fact can serve to excuse future episodes of related negative conduct. The problem from a therapeutic standpoint is that truths, half-truths, and utter false-hoods are woven into the fabric of a mollification, thereby shielding it from the light of objective scrutiny and turning an intervention into a debate over differences of opinion. To avoid the political and philosophical diversion techniques that often accompany mollification, therapists would be well advised to approach this thinking style from the standpoint that it is irrational to use someone else's immoral, illegal, or unethical actions to justify or excuse one's own irresponsible behavior.

Mollification comes in several forms. Yochelson and Samenow (1976) refer to one popular expression of mollification as the "victim stance." Persons utilizing this version of mollification seek to assuage guilt and anxiety consequential to drug or criminal activity by adopting the mind-set that they had no choice but to participate in these activities because they were and still are victims of nefarious social-environmental conditions. Whether the culprits are made out to be the media, government, or their own early home environments, persons committed to a drug or criminal lifestyle are adept at shifting blame onto others as a tactic for avoiding responsibility for their own actions.

A second way in which mollification is commonly expressed is through minimization of harm done to oneself and others. An adolescent well acquainted with the drug lifestyle may justify her consumption of drugs by selectively pointing to research in support of her belief that drugs do no long-term damage to the human body. Mollification is also present in the thinking of an offender who minimizes the seriousness of a criminal act such as bank robbery by inferring that because he never used a weapon (though it may have been displayed), no one was harmed. By discounting any psychological trauma he may have caused the patrons and staff of the bank, such an offender has adopted a narrow definition of harm (i.e., actual physical injury) as a way of counteracting feelings of guilt that sometimes occur as a consequence of involvement in a serious criminal act.

A third common form of mollification involves normalizing one's negative behavior. A juvenile arrested for auto theft may normalize his conduct by pointing out that all of his friends—in fact, everyone he knows—engage in this behavior. The only difference between him and everyone else is that he was unfortunate enough to get caught. The implication here is that because rule-violating behavior is common, the individual is somehow excused from his own criminal actions. Persons committed to a drug lifestyle also rely on normalization as a means of mollifying irresponsibility and drug use, as in the following example:

> John began smoking marijuana and ingesting amphetamine pills (white cross) while still in grade school. It was his contention that "everyone used drugs" and so there couldn't possibly be anything wrong with this behavior. He especially enjoyed introducing novices to marijuana and other drugs as a means of justifying his own use of these same substances. He reasoned that if a significant portion of his peer group used these substances, some of whom were good students, then there couldn't possibly be any harm in his using these substances himself. By age 18, John began selling marijuana in an effort to support his growing dependency on cocaine, and one of his favorite rationalizations was that he was just a merchant providing people with a product they wanted. "After all," he asserted, "if I didn't sell it to them, someone else would."

Criminal mollification is sometimes expressed in the form of transferring blame to the victim. This maneuver is based on the concept of a just world (Lerner, 1970) and consequent belief that if something bad happens to someone, particularly another person, than that person must have deserved it:

> Robert was a longtime bank robber who delighted in jumping over the teller counter when robbing a bank. When confronted in therapy with the realization that this behavior may have created psychological problems for the people in the banks he robbed, particularly the tellers, he stated that he never intended to hurt anyone and that if they suffered psychological problems as a result of the robberies it was because they were weak people who would have suffered psychological problems anyway. He would follow this up by asserting that the tellers should have known the risks associated with working in a bank when they were hired, and so if they suffered any long-term negative effects it was their own fault.

Cutoff

Like most people, drug abusers and criminals are responsive to deterrents. Unlike the average person, however, someone committed to a drug or criminal lifestyle has developed the capacity to eliminate deterrents quickly from consideration. This is what Yochelson and Samenow (1976) refer to as the "cutoff." Lifestyle theory also uses the term *implosion* to describe this particular style of thought because it seems to capture more precisely the flood of anger and emotion that characterizes the cutoff process. It has been observed that persons invested in a drug or criminal lifestyle typically have trouble dealing effectively with stress and frustration (Black & Gregson, 1973). Under such circumstances the individual is apt to rely on implosion to eliminate fears, anxieties, and other deterrents to irresponsible action. There are two primary forms of implosion available to the individual: internal cutoffs, such as a simple phrase, image, or musical theme; and external cutoffs, such as drugs and alcohol.

The phrase most often used by those involved in drug use and criminal activity to eradicate the influence of deterrents is "Fuck it." The anger that fuels this particular feature of implosive cognition rises to a crescendo as the individual feels overwhelmed by stress and frustration; this subsequently contributes to a buildup of tension, which then encourages activation of the "fuck it" mentality, which cuts off deterrents to irresponsible or criminal action. This process is illustrated in the following case example:

> Julie was a long-term heroin addict who for the first time in her life wanted to adopt a drug-free lifestyle. However, because she lacked certain basic social, cognitive, and life management skills she continued to encounter frustration and negative feelings. The first several times she was able to avoid successfully the temptation to use heroin, but eventually the pressure and anger got to be too much and she heard herself say, "Fuck it." The automatic thoughts and behaviors associated with her past drug use then took over and before she knew it she was fixing a syringe with heroin and sticking it into one of the few good veins she had left.

Internal cutoffs can also take the form of mental images or musical themes. Whether the image is positive or negative, it serves the same function as the simple phrase: namely, to implode deterrents to drug use or crime. The use of a musical theme to obliterate deterrents to criminal action is demonstrated in this case vignette:

Rick had committed dozens of convenience store robberies prior to being arrested and placed in a state penitentiary. However, experience had done very little to settle the fear that gripped him each time he entered a convenience store for the purpose of robbery. Over the years, he had developed a technique designed to eradicate the fear and anxiety that normally precedes a criminal act and prevents most people from engaging in this type activity. This technique consisted of subvocally humming a few bars of theme music from a popular western TV show. In less than five seconds, Rick would feel in complete control of his fears and had no trouble conducting a successful robbery. Twenty years later, Rick still gets butterflies in his stomach whenever he enters a convenience store, but now, rather than eliminating these feelings, he employs them as a reminder of where his life would be had he not abandoned the criminal lifestyle.

Though implosion is an internalized cognitive process, it is clearly responsive to external stimuli. Drugs and alcohol are two such stimuli. Criminally inclined subjects may use alcohol to elicit a false sense of courage, heroin to calm their nerves before committing a crime, or cocaine to make themselves feel more alert and invulnerable. The bottom line, however, is that in each case the drug is used to eradicate the fears, anxieties, and uncertainties that under normal circumstances would dissuade the individual from engaging in criminal activity. In interviews conducted with 30 active burglars, Paul Cromwell and his associates (1991) determined that their subjects often consumed alcohol, smoked marijuana, or ingested heroin to eliminate fear and anxiety before burglarizing a residence. Drugs may also serve a cutoff function in the case of future drug use, as exemplified by the individual who plans to limit him- or herself to two drinks and ends up imbibing five times that much on the strength of the implosive value of the first two drinks. This is referred to by practitioners and investigators in the substance abuse field as a "priming effect" (Bradley et al., 1989).

Entitlement

Whereas mollification is used to justify drug and criminal behavior after the fact, entitlement furnishes the individual with permission to engage in such activities in the first place. Entitlement, which has its basis in the egocentricity of childhood, is marked by a global sense of ownership or privilege (Hook & Cook, 1979). Most people eventually abandon this primitive sense of entitlement, though they may harbor circumscribed expressions of entitlement even into adulthood. The drug and criminal lifestyles, on the other hand, give rise to a global sense of entitlement that knows no bounds and typically does not respond to corrective feedback. Consequently, the entitlement associated with the drug and criminal lifestyles differs from the periodic entitlement expressed by a non-drug abuser or noncriminal in both degree and scope.

Three attitudes serve as the framework for entitlement: ownership, uniqueness, and the misidentification of wants as needs. *Ownership* refers to the fact that persons involved in a drug or criminal lifestyle do not respect social boundaries or the personal space of others. Many times these individuals do not realize that they have harmed other people, because they believe they are entitled to act in whatever manner they deem fit. Feeney (1986) reports that many of the robbers he interviewed insisted that there was nothing wrong with their behavior because they were simply recovering funds owed them. The stance assumed by many offenders upon their release from prison also reflects a clear attitude of entitlement:

> As he prepared to leave prison after serving 9 years of a 20-year sentence for rape, Bruce knew exactly what he was going to do. He would look up a number of old friends and then they would have one of the longest-running parties in recorded history. After all, hadn't he just spent nearly 10 years of his life confined in a state penitentiary, away from the people he cared about and called family? He reasoned that society "owed him" and that he was entitled to a good time. It was not long before Bruce was back in custody, facing charges of attempting to rape an off-duty policewoman.

Persons committed to a drug or criminal lifestyle are the curators of the double standard. Hence, although many criminal offenders see the need for law enforcement, they do not think that the law should restrict their own activities; many such individuals genuinely believe that they are above the laws and dictates of society. A drug abuser or serious criminal may express irritation with a younger sibling who verbalizes an interest in using drugs or helping out with a criminal act, but see nothing wrong with engaging in these activities him- or herself. This last point reflects not only entitlement but two additional thinking patterns as well—sentimentality (being the "good guy" by steering a younger sibling away from negative behaviors) and superoptimism (continuing to engage in negative behaviors on the strength of the belief that one can "get away with it"). Feelings of *uniqueness* and privilege can often be traced to early experiences within the home, where the person has been made to feel special, extraordinary, or superior to other children. Though these early experiences do not cause the entitlement thinking associated with a drug or criminal lifestyle, they may facilitate the evolution of this thinking style by instilling an attitude of being above the rules that govern other people's behavior.

A third cognitive trend encompassed by the more general concept of entitlement is the *misidentification of wants as needs*. As a means of procuring permission to use drugs and to violate the rules of society, persons committed to a drug or criminal lifestyle excuse their conduct on the grounds that their actions are driven by needs over which they have no voluntary control. Criminally involved persons often convince themselves that they "need" the money they obtain illegally in order to finance a new car, take a vacation, or keep up with the latest clothing trends in a gratuitous effort to justify the act prior to its commission. The misidentification of wants as needs is frequently a part of the entitlement expressed by persons involved in a drug lifestyle as well:

> Mary had begun using tranquilizers such as Valium and Librium during college as a way of dealing with the anxiety she experienced in both social and academic situations. After college, she took a job as an advertising executive and increased her use of tranquilizers to combat the rising pressure that accompanied this high-profile job. She held this position for six years, until both the pressure and the drug use got to be too much, at which point she quit her job and entered a drug rehabilitation program. It was not until she gave up the belief, based in entitlement, that she needed the drugs to function "normally" that she truly began to enter the early stages of recovery.

When people convince themselves that they need something, they are, in effect, granting themselves permission to do whatever it takes to satisfy that need. The separation of wants from needs is consequently an important step in the change process.

Power Orientation

Low self-esteem is common to the drug and criminal lifestyles. Given that drug- and crime-involved persons are oriented toward the external environment, it makes good intuitive sense that their moods should shift in response to changing environmental contingencies. When such persons are in control of a situation they feel potent, virile, and exhilarated. Feeney's (1986) robbers, for instance, expressed sentiments showing that they found robbing people at gunpoint to be a very rewarding and gratifying experience. David McClelland and his associates have determined that many heavy drinkers display power-oriented interests and fantasies designed, perhaps, to compensate for inner feelings of worthlessness and fear (McClelland, Davis, Kalin, & Wanner, 1972). Paul J. Goldstein (1981) reports that hustling and copping behaviors not only provide heroin addicts with a source of income but also promote a sense of environmental control and influence that can become self-reinforcing over time. Power is therefore seen as an important motivator of both drug and criminal lifestyle activities.

When an individual who places a premium on external control fails to exert control over an environmental event or situation, he or she is faced with what Yochelson and Samenow (1976) refer to as the "zero state." *Physically impotent, weak,* and *powerless* are adjectives commonly used to describe the zero-state experience. Settings where drug addicts and criminals are commonly found, including jails, prisons, and drunk tanks, elicit zero-state feelings by illustrating just how little control the individual has over his or her immediate environment. Zero-state feelings are typically eliminated by thoughts and actions designed to take control of a situation, a phenomenon known as "power thrusting" (Yochelson & Samenow, 1976). The power orientation, therefore, comprises two interrelated processes: the zero state and the power thrust. Some individuals have become so sensitive to zero-state feelings that they power thrust at the first hint of a negative affective state and give the appearance of power thrusting for no apparent reason. It is the contention of lifestyle theory, however, that the zero state and power thrust go hand in hand, and that nearly all power thrusts can be traced back to a stimulatory zero state.

The power thrust can be expressed in several forms, the most obvious being physical. Here the individual either physically assaults another person or engages in property destruction. The verbal power thrust is characterized by frequent arguments and conversations designed to put someone else down or make oneself appear to be more intelligent or educated than is actually the case. The mental power thrust entails reworking a situation over in one's mind so that one comes out on top and someone else is embarrassed or humiliated. Though the mental power thrust may reflect greater self-control then either the physical or verbal power thrust, it is by no means a satisfactory response to zero-state feelings in that, like the physical and verbal power thrusts, it reinforces the bond between the zero state and the power thrust. Until the individual learns to cope with zero-state feelings in ways other than by power thrusting, he or she will continue to be victimized by his or her irrational power-seeking behavior. This is clearly delineated in the following case history:

Tim was a 15-year-old bully who sought to exert power and control over his environment at every turn. It got to the point where his parents could no longer control his behavior and had him admitted to a treatment unit for behaviorally disordered juveniles. A disruptive influence on the unit, Tim would regularly put other residents down and would take positions in arguments that not even he agreed with. He argued simply to be in control of situations, and he rarely "lost" an argument because he wouldn't stay around long enough to hear the other person's point of view. Furthermore, if there was something he wanted he would simply take it. On the unit he would intimidate and threaten and, in the rare instances when this did not get him his way, he would become physically aggressive, punching a wall if the conflict was with a staff person or assaulting the other person if the conflict was with a peer.

Power thrusts do not always follow along the physical-verbal-mental continuum. Within the context of the drug lifestyle, the power thrust can be seen as an attempt by the individual to gain a sense of control over his or her feeling state through the use of mood-altering substances. The specific mood a drug promotes may be less important than the fact that the drug facilitates a change in mood. The power thrust can also be visual, in the sense that it might involve attracting attention to oneself through the clothing one wears or the way one acts. Sometimes the power thrust is symbolic, as displayed in the actions of the 42-year-old female who serves as the subject of the next case vignette:

A product of the Woodstock generation, Winny had spent the past 25 years in and out of various drug treatment facilities with very little success. It did not bother her that many of her friends and family considered her a "dope fiend," a label that, in fact, she seemed to regard with a certain degree of pride. Winny went out of her way to attract attention to herself through the unusual, outdated clothes she wore and the company she kept. This, however, did nothing to alleviate the depression and powerlessness she felt when she could not control her life. Eventually she engaged in the ultimate power thrust, overdosing on a combination of tranquilizers, cocaine, and heroin.

In addition to providing the individual with constructive ways of managing zero-state feelings, treatment needs to work toward a reorientation of thinking in which external control is no longer valued above all else and is gradually replaced by a more realistic control goal, that of self-discipline.

Sentimentality

Because some of the actions in which people engage are incompatible with the positive images they may have fashioned for themselves, they must find ways to reconcile obvious discrepancies between their behavior and their positive self-views. One way this might be accomplished is through a thinking style known as sentimentality (Yochelson & Samenow, 1976). Though all humans display sentimentality from time to time, persons involved in a drug or criminal lifestyle must often go to greater lengths in atoning for their behavior because their transgressions are usually more extreme and the consequences ostensibly more far-reaching than those of the average citizen. Like mollification, sentimentality is designed to justify behavior after its occurrence; however, whereas mollification entails justification on the basis of various environmental considerations, sentimentality involves justification on the basis of one's own abilities and good nature. The white-collar offenders interviewed by Benson (1985) utilized both mollification and sentimentality to neutralize guilt brought on by their violations of societal rules. Bennett's (1986) heroin addicts did much the same thing in justifying their involvement in a drug lifestyle.

Sentimentality, as it pertains to a drug or criminal lifestyle, consists of a self-centered attempt by the individual to pattern and promote a positive image of him- or herself, thereby denying, ignoring, or trivializing the negative consequences of his or her lifestyle decision. Drug abusers and criminals frequently focus their sentimentality on the small, the injured, and the helpless. Thus defenseless children, wounded animals, and infirm elders are often the beneficiaries of drug abusers' or criminals' self-centered attempts to project positive personal images. With the hospitalized drug abuser or the incarcerated criminal, sentimentality often takes the form of concern for the patient's or inmate's family or children, although prior to the separation many such individuals have little time for their families because their priorities lie elsewhere. This exposes the selfish core and false nature of sentimentality, a fact that is borne out further in the following case vignette:

> Mike had a long history of alcohol abuse that had been a source of embarrassment and turmoil for his wife and three young children.

However, in Mike's own mind he was the consummate family man. He would tell himself that his family never had to apply for welfare and that he always attended his children's birthday parties, even if he had to interrupt a drinking binge to be there. Mike never really understood the psychological pain he put his family through until he was confronted by his wife and kids in a particularly intensive session of family therapy that had been set up through the employee assistance program sponsored by Mike's employer.

Sentimentality may also appear in an aesthetic or artistic form, as represented by an individual's involvement with art, music, or literature. The problem with these particular expressions of sentimentality is that although a person may dabble in these activities from time to time—chiefly when hospitalized or incarcerated—he or she frequently loses interest in these diversions once the opportunity for more immediate and self-indulgent activities appears as a consequence of release back to the community:

> Jim was an accomplished artist, or at least so he thought. While in prison, he would spend much of his time in the recreation department, painting landscapes that he either imagined in his mind or saw in books and magazines. He would brag to other inmates that he was going to be a professional painter upon his release from prison and that he had several offers from galleries for his paintings. Whether this was true or not, upon his release from prison Jim abandoned painting, professional or otherwise, and began writing bad checks to cover the lavish lifestyle of drugs, women, and fun to which he believed he was entitled. On his return to prison after only six months in the community, Jim resumed his painting career as if he had never left.

One question often raised when the topic of sentimentality is broached is how to discriminate between sentimentality and true caring and concern. The most obvious difference is that sentimentality is selfish and ego centered, whereas genuine social concern is selfless and other centered. Most people display both sentimentality and true concern, and many actions subsume a combination of the two. However, it should be pointed out that sentimentality cannot be distinguished from genuine care and concern with any degree of accuracy or confidence except by the individual him- or herself. The goal of intervention is to assist clients in coming to terms with their negative behavior by instructing them in ways in which they might strip away the sentimentality that clouds their self-awareness and inhibits their will to change. Without active intervention directed specifically at sentimentality, the client, in all likelihood, will continue to view him- or herself as a good person who does no real harm to others and therefore requires no change in behavior.

Superoptimism

Superoptimism consists of an unrealistic appraisal of one's ability to avoid the negative consequences of one's behavior (Yochelson & Samenow, 1976). Though grounded in fantasy, superoptimism, at least initially, is based on several facts. It is a fact, for instance, that criminals get away with the majority of their offenses. When we consider that roughly half of all crimes go unreported (Eck & Riccio, 1979) and that only 52% of the violent crimes and 16% of the property crimes reported to police are actually cleared by arrest (Maguire & Flanagan, 1991), we can see that offenders have a 75% chance of getting away with a serious violent crime and a 92% chance of getting away with a significant property crime. Similarly, because of the remarkable recuperative powers of the human body and the resilience of the human spirit, the average individual can consume large quantities of alcohol and other drugs and not neces-sarily experience the negative consequences of the drug lifestyle for many months or even years. The result is that superoptimism devel-ops as a consequence of involvement in a drug or criminal lifestyle in which early success encourages the taking of even greater risks on the strength of the belief that one will be able to avoid the negative consequences of this lifestyle indefinitely.

Most criminals realize that there is a chance they will eventually get caught (Katz, 1979), but most convince themselves that it will not be at the present time. As a case in point, only 21% of the robbers interviewed by Feeney (1986) considered apprehension a risk they should concern themselves with in planning their most recent rob-bery. This superoptimistic attitude tends to grow with experience in a criminal lifestyle, as shown in a study by R. A. Siegel (1978). Siegel discerned that psychopathic and nonpsychopathic offenders achieved comparable results on a card-sorting task when the probability of punishment was very high or very low, but that the group high in psychopathy (a concept that seems to parallel the criminal lifestyle in many respects) achieved significantly lower winnings and substan-tially lower response suppression when the probability of punish-ment was uncertain. Siegel interprets these findings as supporting a cognitive interpretation of criminal behavior in which magical and superstitious thinking predominates in persons who show clear allegiance to a criminal lifestyle (i.e., psychopathic offenders). The self-destructive aspects of superoptimism are depicted in the following case vignette:

> Sarah had never held a legitimate job for longer than two weeks, and she was informed by her probation officer that if she violated the conditions of her probation one more time she would be spending the next six months in jail. Her voracious appetite for benzodiazepine (Xanax) and opioids (Dilaudid) had led her into a number of illegal activities, including shoplifting and periodic work as a prostitute. With each successful shoplifting escapade she became increasingly self-confident, to the point that she stopped taking even basic precautions. It was not long before she was apprehended attempting to boost a television set from a large department store, when the set's cord dropped from beneath the oversized dress she was wearing to conceal the item. The police were unsympathetic to her protestations that she would never engage in this behavior again and took her to the police station for booking.

Just as it is important to discriminate between sentimentality and true care and concern, it is vital that the individual be able to distinguish between superoptimism and a healthy sense of self-confidence. Self-confidence and normal optimism are based in reality and help to direct individuals toward realistic goals; superoptimism is based in fantasy and is unproductive because it deceives individuals into believing they can realize fantastic goals with minimal effort. Needless to say, although the superoptimistic individual may succeed for a period of time, his or her luck will eventually run out, which in the end only makes the ultimate failure that much more dramatic and tragic. Such was the case with Jerome, the subject of the next case vignette:

> Jerome was a 19-year-old PCP smoker when he was brought into the hospital emergency room in a quasi-psychotic state. Several days later, when he was more coherent, he described his descent into a drug lifestyle. He had seen friends and acquaintances suffering personal, family, and physical problems as a consequence of their use of PCP and other drugs, but he kept telling himself that it couldn't happen to him because he could control his use of drugs. Of course, the fact that he had used PCP 30 or 40 times before he had his first negative experience simply added to the superoptimism that seemed to grow each time he used drugs. It would take several more trips to the hospital emergency room for Jerome to realize that each time he ingested PCP he was gambling with his future; he eventually abandoned the drug lifestyle and entered college.

Cognitive Indolence

Persons initially involved in a drug or criminal lifestyle may tend to be cautious in evaluating drug or criminal opportunities. Over time, however, these individuals become progressively lazier and more uncritical of their thoughts and plans. Warning signs they may have heeded in the past are now ignored or overlooked as the individuals move into the more advanced stages of a drug or criminal lifestyle. Reasoning powers are directed at achieving the swiftest possible results, regardless of what this might mean in the long run. Shortcut thinking also becomes increasingly prevalent as commitment to a drug or criminal lifestyle grows. Because of the lazy, uncritical approach adopted by most early- and advanced-stage drug abusers and criminals in the face of everyday problems, their lives get out of control rather quickly. Though they may find short-term solutions to their problems, their myopic approach to problem solving eventually creates even more serious problems for them in the long run.

Drugs may alleviate anxiety, stress, and frustration for a brief period of time, but they rarely solve the long-term problems that plague those who misuse drugs. Continued drug abuse subsequently leads to further deterioration of these persons' abilities to think critically and solve problems effectively. In this respect, drugs are both a cause and an effect of cognitive indolence. The end result is an individual who has difficulty conducting an objective review of his or her behavior and who generally comes across as lazy and irresponsible in interpersonal situations:

> Samantha enjoyed the effect marijuana had on her behavior, and she would while away the hours smoking this substance with a small circle of friends. When high on marijuana, she and her friends would discuss their plans for the future, though they often neglected the details and logistics of how they might carry these plans out in a realistic fashion. Nearly everyone in the group had rejected family, work, and financial responsibilities. Responsibility was particularly frightening to Samantha—so frightening, in fact, that she entered a treatment program so that she would not lose her social security benefits. However, she dropped out of treatment after several days because, she said, she viewed it as irrelevant to her situation and life goals. In reality, she didn't want to invest the energy required to complete the program successfully. Samantha rationalized that nobody in society cared and went back to the only place where she felt accepted—her small circle of pot-smoking friends.

The thinking of persons involved in drug and criminal lifestyles often gravitates toward "get-rich-quick" schemes because many such individuals desire material success but do not wish to invest the time and effort required to attain it through legitimate channels. Even in situations where they might benefit from adopting a more critical attitude, persons affiliated with a drug or criminal lifestyle characteristically assume a lazy or nonvigilant attitude. In one study, in which a group of incarcerated offenders was exposed to an aversive one-second tone, 90% selected a nonvigilant approach to a task (listening to a nightclub comic) when the aversive tone could not be avoided. However, when the tone could be avoided, 75% of the sample continued with the nonvigilant mode despite the fact that a vigilant attitude would have aided them in terminating the aversive stimulus (Hare, 1982). Nonvigilance is epitomized in the following case vignette:

> Jake was serving a six-month sentence in a federal prison camp for embezzling money from the fast-food restaurant where he worked while attending a local college. With a measured IQ of 125 and a pleasing disposition, Jake had what it took to be a success. However, lack of effort, procrastination, and a nonvigilant approach to situations had left him 36 credits short of a bachelor's degree after four years of college. He subsequently left the university to work in the auto industry. Though he drew a good salary, he soon became bored and quit. After several months of wandering through the American Southwest, he returned to his hometown near Detroit, where he enrolled part-time in a local college program and went to work at a fast-food restaurant. Always one to take advantage of shortcut opportunities, Jake began to steal money from the cash register until one day, because of nonvigilance, he was literally caught with his hand in the till.

In working with a client who has a problem with nonvigilance and cognitive indolence, a useful intervention technique is to pin the individual down to specifics. Because cognitive indolence, like the other seven thinking styles, is a patterned thought process, it continues to evolve as the lifestyle unfolds. Statements such as "I'll get to it tomorrow" and "It will eventually work out" reflect the lack of critical reasoning found in cognitive indolence, a pattern that will continue to prosper if such statements are not challenged. Cognitive indolence impedes the change process by providing an escape hatch for the negative self-statements that serve the drug and criminal lifestyles. Persons in a drug or criminal lifestyle must be confronted when they procrastinate, opposed when they take shortcuts, and made to be more specific when they offer vague generalities in place of concrete strategies and plans. Without such corrective action, cognitive indolence will continue to grow and the individual will have no reason to challenge his or her lazy, irresponsible thinking.

Discontinuity

Just because someone involved in a drug or criminal lifestyle desires and pursues change is no guarantee that change will occur. Drug- and crime-involved subjects are inclined to lose sight of long-term goals in their single-minded pursuit of immediate gratification and the exploration of drug and criminal opportunities. Even if the individual actively rejects the immediate gratification of drugs and crime, he or she must still overcome years of prior learning in which short-term desires have been placed ahead of long-term goals. Learning new ways to cope with life situations can be an extremely arduous task and one that requires a great deal more patience, perseverance, and effort than a person currently or previously committed to a drug or criminal lifestyle is used to exercising. Hence such an individual will display inconsistency, lack of focus, and poor goal attainment, because he or she lacks internal direction and self-discipline. This is what lifestyle theorists refer to as discontinuity.

The lack of persistence and the unpredictability that characterize drug and criminal lifestyles can be traced back to early developmental factors. As Werner (1957) has postulated, the human organism moves from a state of global undifferentiation, to one of differentiation, to one of integration. The young child is, by nature, discontinuous. The inattention of infancy occurs because the organism cannot differentiate itself from the external environment. With differentiation comes further movement away from this primitive state of egocentricity, although it is not until the individual achieves integration that he or she develops true autonomy. A person at risk for future problems of either a drug or criminal nature is viewed to be less autonomous and more externally oriented than those who do not abuse drugs or engage in serious criminality (Buikhuisen, Bontekoe, Plas-Korenhoff, & van Buuren, 1984). This external orientation not only places the individual at increased risk for future drug and criminal outcomes but also makes the individual more susceptible to environmental distraction:

Maria began using alcohol and marijuana when she was 14. By age 16 she had added crack cocaine and the psychostimulant ice to the list of drugs she imbibed regularly. She would talk a great deal about her plans for the future, but rarely followed through on these intentions. During these conversations Maria would jump around from subject to subject, making it difficult for others to understand her and leading many of them to avoid her altogether. Feeling isolated, Maria sought solace at crack houses, where her use of crack and ice only served to make her thoughts and actions even more discontinuous and fragmented.

The lack of integration that gives rise to an external orientation also facilitates the development of a process known as compartmentalization. A child naturally compartmentalizes seemingly incompatible experiences. An individual who never fully realizes the integration stage of human cognitive development is therefore at risk for engaging in extensive compartmentalization during adulthood. Compartmentalization lends itself to future drug and criminal outcomes because it provides the individual with the opportunity to isolate, and therefore avoid, the responsibilities associated with adult living. Consequently, the individual does not have to deal with the less savory aspects of his or her behavior because they can be neatly and conveniently classified as uncharacteristic anomalies ("not me"). Of course, although compartmentalization and the external orientation may have their roots in early developmental experiences, both evolve further in support of a drug or criminal lifestyle because they are convenient ways of evading responsibility for one's actions.

With regard to intervention, discontinuity interferes with a person's ability to carry out initially good intentions, because, although the individual may desire change at a specific point in time, he or she has difficulty maintaining this commitment in the face of shifting environmental contingencies. The external orientation and compartmentalization that form the basis of discontinuity aggravate the individual's vulnerability to negative life events because he or she is unable to exercise control over his or her behavior because of a lack of both integration and cognitive maturity. This is explicitly displayed in the following case vignette:

When he was released from prison for the second time, Roland told himself that he would never forget the prison experience and would use the memory of it to avoid any future legal problems. Prison soon faded from memory, however, as Roland became familiar once again with life on the streets. Within two weeks Roland's conception of prison was

nothing more than a surrealistic nightmare that had no impact whatso-
ever on his behavior. It was not long before he was back in trouble and
back in prison.

This unfortunately all-too-familiar story captures the attitudes and
beliefs of many persons who leave prison with the best of intentions
but wind up in trouble shortly thereafter because they lack the skills
and perseverance necessary to achieve long-term success. Confront-
ing the discontinuity of the drug and criminal lifestyles is therefore
an important step in any program of intervention designed to
convert good intentions into realistic action.

Conclusion

It is clear that drug and criminal lifestyles are supported by a
common set of beliefs. However, just because these lifestyles share
the same eight thinking patterns does not mean that the cognitive
features associated with drug and criminal involvement are identical.
Thinking tends to vary as a function of the behavior it is designed
to support and promote. Mollifications indigenous to a drug lifestyle
are invented for the purpose of legitimizing patterned drug use and
the irresponsibility that often accompanies such use, whereas mollifications that are part of a criminal lifestyle are formed in an effort
to justify angry feelings by finding fault with others or with society
in general. Likewise, the power orientation observed in a drug
lifestyle concerns the individual's need to gain a sense of control over
his or her mood and the drug use venue, whereas in a criminal setting
the power orientation has to do with attaining power and control
over others. When it comes right down to it, however, mollification,
power orientation, and the other six thinking patterns are more
similar than they are different when compared across the drug and
criminal lifestyles, and they go a long way toward explaining the
drug-crime overlap.

It should be noted that the eight thinking patterns respond to both
developmental and experiential contingencies. As I have pointed out
several times in this chapter, the eight thinking patterns have their
roots in early developmental issues. Persons who encounter difficulty with what lifestyle theorists refer to as the early life tasks
(Person × Situation interactions) are placed at increased risk for
future drug and criminal outcomes. By the same token, environmental experiences may also place a person at increased risk for

future drug and criminal involvement by supporting one or more of the eight thinking patterns. The power orientation, for instance, is inspired by early interactions in an environment where physical prowess and power are prized over intellectual acumen. A certain percentage of persons exposed to this type environment, and a smaller percentage of persons not so exposed, will then elect to engage in drug and crime activities sufficient to enter into the early stages of lifestyle development.

Experiential contingencies enter the picture as the individual begins to form a commitment to a drug or criminal lifestyle and gradually finds it necessary to justify and rationalize his or her lifestyle-based activities. Occasionally, this experiential effect is a direct consequence of a drug or criminal event; for example, the pharmacological action of cocaine may directly stimulate the development of grandiosity and the thinking pattern of superoptimism. More often, however, the experiential effect can be traced to actual involvement in lifestyle activities, as is the case with cognitive indolence, which tends to grow as the individual avoids adult responsibilities. In understanding the drug-crime connection it is important, therefore, to remember that as a drug or criminal lifestyle evolves, the thinking patterns that support this lifestyle become increasingly intertwined and mutually dependent. Consequently, during the more advanced stages of lifestyle development, expressions of one thinking pattern tend to activate one or more other thinking patterns, which, in turn, facilitate a cross-fertilization of related lifestyles such as those that sustain drug and criminal activity.

5. Change

The overriding purpose of lifestyle intervention is to stimulate, promote, and enlist a client's adaptive resources. Whereas a drug or criminal lifestyle encourages entrenchment, adaptation fosters change. Lifestyle intervention branches off into two distinct tracts, also known as the structural and functional models of intervention. The present discussion is organized around the structural model, the three primary goals of which are (a) to modify and manage current-contextual conditions, (b) to accentuate choice options and decision-making competence, and (c) to identify and challenge irrational and self-defeating forms of ideation as a means of generating rational alternatives to drug- and criminal-activity-oriented thinking.

Condition-Based Change Strategies

Based on research showing that current-contextual conditions may have greater relevance to the drug-crime connection than historical-developmental conditions, the present discussion will examine ways in which current-contextual conditions might be effectively managed. Negative affect, interoceptive and exteroceptive cues, availability, and interpersonal situations have been implicated as important in relapse to both drug abuse (Bradley et al., 1989; Marlatt, 1978) and crime (Cusson & Pinsonneault, 1986; West & Farrington, 1973). Research suggests that a variety of different techniques might be useful in managing current-contextual conditions, but affect regulation, cue control, access reduction, relationship modification, and substitution are the procedures that have the greatest level of documented efficacy in this regard.

Affect Regulation

It has been proposed that stress causes negative affect, which, in turn, elevates the risk of relapse in persons who customarily alleviate stress-linked negative affect by ingesting chemicals (self-medication) or engaging in other forms of acting-out behavior (e.g., delinquency and crime). Analyzing 311 relapse episodes suffered by treated alcoholics, heroin addicts, cigarette smokers, overeaters, and compulsive gamblers, Cummings, Gordon, and Marlatt (1980) discerned that negative emotional states (depression, anger, and frustration) accounted for 35% of the relapses suffered by these subjects. The retrospective accounts of 30 inpatients enrolled in an alcohol treatment program revealed that negative emotional states such as anger/frustration and depression accounted for 47% of the initial lapses and 80% of the reported episodes of drug use following the initial lapse (Schonfeld, Rohrer, Dupree, & Thomas, 1989). Cusson and Pinsonneault (1986) ascertained that depression, boredom, and frustration were important in encouraging the resumption of criminal activity in a group of ex-offenders who had been living crime-free in the community for several years. Pithers et al. (1983) surmised that anger and a desire for power brought on by negative life events were important themes in the reports of rapists who relapsed, whereas depression and isolation were more common precipitants of relapse in pedophiles.

Given that negative affect appears to be largely a consequence of environmental stress, the logical approach to treatment would be to instruct drug abusers and criminals in such stress management techniques as relaxation training, exercise, assertiveness, and anger control. The stress-reducing properties and capabilities of relaxation training (Davidson & Schwartz, 1976), meditation (Shapiro &

Walsh, 1984), and biofeedback (Khatami, Mintz, & O'Brien, 1978) are well documented. The applicability of these procedures to the treatment of drug abuse and criminality remains an open question, but there is some evidence that relaxation training (Marlatt & Marques, 1977), biofeedback (Denney, Baugh, & Hardt, 1991), aerobic exercise (Murphy, Pagano, & Marlatt, 1986), and assertiveness training (Chaney, O'Leary, & Marlatt, 1978) may be of some assistance to persons attempting to extricate themselves from a drug lifestyle, and that desensitization (Bancroft, 1970) and role-playing procedures (Sarason, 1968) may be of some value in preventing former offenders from relapsing into a criminal lifestyle.

Cue Control

Just as negative affect can be attributed to stressful life events, urges, cravings, and withdrawal symptoms are largely a consequence of exteroceptive (external) and interoceptive (internal) stimuli or cues. The opponent process model of tolerance and withdrawal symptomatology imputes the subjective experience of craving to exteroceptive (external) cues that elicit a drug-opposite or compensatory effect designed to prepare the organism for drug ingestion (S. Siegel, 1988). Consistent with this viewpoint, research shows that alcohol has a stronger effect on heart rate (Drafters & Anderson, 1982) and cognitive functioning (Shapiro & Nathan, 1986) when it is served in settings not typically associated with alcohol consumption, presumably because many of the ethanol-related cues known to give rise to a drug-opposite effect are absent. The fact that heroin addicts and patients prescribed morphine have overdosed on opiate levels they had previously been able to tolerate when using these substances in an unfamiliar setting is further evidence in support of the validity of the opponent process model of drug tolerance and withdrawal symptomatology (Siegel, Hinson, Krank, & McCully, 1982).

Interoceptive and exteroceptive cues may be as important in the evolution of a criminal lifestyle as they are in the development of a drug lifestyle. Pithers, Kashima, Cumming, Beal, and Buell (1987), for instance, determined that 69% of the rapists and 57% of the pedophiles they studied displayed deviant sexual preference as measured by the penile plethysmograph (a commonly employed instrument for measuring sexual arousal), with rapists exhibiting greater arousal to visual depictions of rape than to scenes of consensual sexual intercourse and pedophiles recording extreme arousal in the presence of child-related cues. In carrying out such research, most investigators indicate partiality toward audiotape procedures, in that they permit greater modification of relevant stimulus parameters (e.g., age of victim, use of force) than do videotape procedures. For this same reason, most clinicians prefer the use of audiotapes in the treatment of sex offenders. It has been noted in clinical research on sex offender groups that the probability of relapse is substantially reduced in situations where the cues associated with the subject's deviant sexual arousal have been addressed through counterconditioning (Quinsey & Marshall, 1983).

There are two basic procedures useful in managing the interoceptive and exteroceptive cues associated with drug abuse and crime: cue avoidance and cue exposure. It is noteworthy that only 12% of the opiate-dependent servicemen detoxified in Vietnam relapsed upon their return to the United States (Robins, Davis, & Goodwin, 1974) in comparison with a 90% rate of relapse in detoxified addicts who are returned to the environments in which they acquired their habits (Cushman, 1974). The remarkably low rate of relapse achieved by returning Vietnam veterans has been ascribed to a change in the stimulus parameters that control drug use: that is, many of the environmental cues that supported heroin use in Vietnam were no longer present once the individuals returned to the United States (S. Siegel, 1986). Consequently, geographic change has been used and found moderately efficacious in controlling relapse in opiate addicts living in Detroit, Michigan (Ross, 1973); San Antonio, Texas (Maddux & Desmond, 1982); and Sweden (Frykholm, 1979). The principal limitation of cue avoidance as an intervention for cue-related craving is that environmental or geographic change is not always possible. For this reason other stimulus control procedures, such as cue exposure, must be considered.

Extinction, or cue exposure, is a behavioral technique wherein the subject is exposed to the cues that elicit craving but is prevented from engaging in the behavior (drug use, crime) that will satisfy the craving. Continued presentation of the cue in the absence of the prohibited behavior leads to a gradual weakening of the cue-behavior bond and a corresponding reduction in urges and craving. Blakey and Baker (1980) exposed persons with past histories of alcohol abuse to a series of alcohol-related cues, such as the sight and smell of ethanol and trips to their favorite pub, without allowing them to drink. After an initial period of increased craving and anxiety, Blakey and Baker discovered that the urge to drink gradually diminished and eventually extinguished altogether. Thinking along parallel lines,

Ronald K. Siegel (1984) presented cocaine-dependent subjects with vials containing a white powdery substance that duplicated the odor and appearance of "street" cocaine. After several trials he noticed that the craving for cocaine began to dwindle, as did drug-seeking behavior. Cue exposure techniques might be most efficacious if utilized in conjunction with a standard regime of treatment, as was observed in a group of cocaine-dependent Veterans Administration patients (O'Brien, Childress, McLellan, & Ehrman, 1990).

A procedure known as masturbatory satiation has proven moderately efficacious in extinguishing the deviant fantasies and aberrant activities of male sex offenders. Therapists utilizing this approach instruct the client to masturbate in the presence of an appropriate stimulus or sexual fantasy (e.g., adult female) to the point of ejaculation. Following ejaculation, the client is advised to continue masturbating for 50 minutes to an hour to the deviant stimulus or fantasy (e.g., prepubescent male). This exposure to a deviant stimulus or fantasy when in a nonaroused state is the extinction phase of the treatment program. If by chance the offender should become aroused to this deviant stimulus or fantasy, he is instructed to switch back immediately to the appropriate imaginal cue. Masturbatory satiation and a related procedure known as verbal satiation have also been found to be effective in the treatment of sexually aberrant behavior (Abel & Annon, 1982), although research on these procedures has been plagued by methodological problems and oversights, ranging from small sample sizes to the presence of numerous uncontrolled influences.

Access Reduction

Having access to drugs or possessing the opportunity to violate the law are necessary prerequisites of drug use and crime. It makes good intuitive sense, then, that limiting a person's access to drugs or criminal opportunities may serve a behavioral management function. The rate of liver cirrhosis (a reasonably good public health indicator of alcohol abuse), for instance, shows reasonably good concordance with the availability of alcohol in cross-national studies on alcoholism (Crowley, 1988). Crowley (1988) found further evidence in favor of an availability-drug abuse nexus when he probed the relationship between prescription drug availability and serious substance abuse. In this study Crowley discerned that prescriptions for pharmaceutical cocaine, benzodiazepine, methaqualone, and other abusable medications were 2 to 17 times more frequent, and the proportion of adults classified as "involved and dysfunctional" drug abusers three to four times more prevalent (24.3% versus 6.8%), in a Colorado ski community compared with the Colorado state average. The fact that many heroin addicts place the availability of opiates near the top of the their lists of reasons for initially using heroin (Simpson & Marsh, 1986) and for relapsing after a period of treatment and/or voluntary abstinence (Meyer & Mirin, 1979) lends further credence to the theory that there is a connection between drug availability and rate of substance abuse.

Availability or access has also been studied with respect to the proposed link between criminal opportunities and outcomes. Brown and Altman (1983) report that burglarized homes exhibit fewer signs of occupancy, fewer physical barriers (locked doors or alarm systems), and fewer psychological or symbolic barriers (fences or warning signs) than do nonburglarized homes. Homeowners in St. Louis (Schimerman, 1974) and Seattle (Seattle Law & Justice Planning Office, 1975) who participated in a target-hardening campaign by marking household items with indelible ink and advertising this fact in a prominent place (e.g., front door, picture window) experienced 25%-33% fewer burglaries than nonparticipating households. Germany and Great Britain implemented opportunity-reducing procedures by equipping new automobiles with locking steering columns, which led to a marked decrease in the theft of new cars (Mayhew, Clarke, Sturman, & Hough, 1976). Research on "defensible space" theory indicates that criminals are also deterred by modifications of architectural design in which the level of surveillance afforded tenants and homeowners is enhanced (MacDonald & Gifford, 1989).

Availability functions on both molar (community/society) and molecular (individual) levels. Financial independence, for example, may facilitate delinquency by providing individual adolescents with premature autonomy from adult control (Cullen et al., 1985). There is also evidence that a sharp rise in financial condition created by participation in a successful criminal venture may promote accelerated drug use in opiate addicts who may have previously maintained themselves on low to moderate doses of heroin (Faupel & Klockars, 1987). These two studies intimate that money may encourage deviant behavior by loosening or destabilizing environmental constraints, such as parental supervision or life structure, that normally discourage substance use and crime, which in the long run leads to an increase in the availability of drug and criminal opportunities. Availability has been shown to be important in initiating substance use during the early stages of drug involvement (Gillmore et al., 1990) and in maintaining such use once the person has entered the advanced stages of a drug or addictive lifestyle (Barrett, Joe, & Simpson, 1990).

Modifying Interpersonal Relationships

Social pressure, including verbal coercion and entering into relationships with persons involved in regular drug use, was the single most powerful determinant of relapse cited by a group of heroin addicts in a study by Marlatt and Gordon (1980). Social influence may also have been operating in a group of criminally persistent English males followed up by West (1982). West notes that a much larger portion of this group was still associating with an all-male peer group at age 18 or 19 in comparison with a group of previously delinquent youth who had successfully abandoned serious criminal behavior. After reviewing 159 separate incidents of homicide and assault, Felson and Steadman (1983) concluded that the perpetrators were frequently responding to verbal attacks by the antagonists/victims, in that serious violence was more prevalent in situations where the antagonists were aggressive or in possession of weapons. In a follow-up to this study, Felson et al. (1984) determined that the perpetrators struck more blows when bystanders, usually friends or family members, supported or encouraged violence than when bystanders attempted to mediate the disputes.

Geographic change has been known to support abstinence and prevent relapse in opiate addicts (Maddux & Desmond, 1982; Ross, 1973), although there is no way to determine with any degree of certainty whether the outcomes of these studies were caused by changes in interpersonal relationships or the evasion of drug-related cues. It stands to reason, however, that if someone were to avoid initiating contact with persons involved in a negative lifestyle, then he or she would have a better chance of remaining drug- or crime-free than someone who maintains regular contact with drug users or active criminal offenders. Cusson and Pinsonneault (1986) note that several of the ex-offenders they interviewed attributed their success in remaining crime-free to the fact that they eschewed prior criminal associations. Of course, dodging prior drug or criminal companions will have little effect if the individual simply replaces these old affiliations with a new group of drug or criminal cohorts. Supplanting lifestyle-based relationships with a supportive network of valued friendships is therefore an essential step in the process of lifestyle change.

Positive interpersonal relationships can be helpful in providing a constructive focus for someone interested in resisting future drug or criminal temptation. Family support, for instance, has been shown to guard against relapse in drug users (Wermuth & Scheidt, 1986) and criminal offenders (Cernkovich & Giordano, 1987). Former alcohol abusers (Tuchfeld, 1981; Vaillant & Milofsky, 1982) and ex-offenders (Irwin, 1970; Shover, 1983) who have abandoned a drug or criminal lifestyle report that their actions were motivated by the formation of new intimate relationships or the reestablishment of old intimate relationships. The development of positive relationships, however, presupposes the capacity for personal responsibility, something that can be learned through behavioral contracting and contingency management procedures. Research suggests that increased personal accountability, as signified by a reduced number of arrests (Douds, Engelsjord, & Collingwood, 1977), decreased drug relapse (Fraser, Hawkins, & Howard, 1988), enhanced commitment to employment (Doctor & Polakow, 1973), and increased responsibility (Douds et al., 1977) are frequently observed in adolescents and young adults taught basic behavioral contracting and contingency management skills.

Substitution

If one is to give up a pleasurable or reinforcing activity, such as drug use or crime, then one must find a suitable replacement. Former drug abusers and offenders are often surprised at how much free time they have once they abandon a drug or criminal lifestyle. They must learn to pack this "spare" time with constructive activities or risk returning to a drug or criminal lifestyle out of boredom. Vaillant and Milofsky (1982) note that nearly half the abstinent men they interviewed had found one or more substitutes for alcohol. In studies of persons who have exited an alcohol-based drug lifestyle without benefit of formal treatment, it has been shown that the availability of and desire for non-alcohol-related substitute activities is an important feature of relapse prevention (Ludwig, 1985; Tuchfeld, 1981). Reviewing the literature on spontaneous remission in persons who had previously abused alcohol, tobacco, or opiates, Stall and Biernacki (1986) determined that craving was characteristically handled by engaging in substitute activities, such as jogging, meditation, or absorption in work.

Cusson and Pinsonneault (1986) report that an interesting and meaningful job was viewed by the ex-offenders in their study as instrumental to their continued avoidance of criminal temptation. Irwin (1970) examined the decisions of 15 male ex-convicts to abandon the criminal lifestyle and determined that consummation of a satisfying relationship with a woman and commitment to extravocational and extradomestic activities were largely responsible for their continued desistance from crime. Certain qualities of a person's leisure-time activities should also be taken into account in determining their value as facilitators or inhibitors of future criminal involvement. Agnew and Petersen (1989) determined that participation in unsupervised peer-related social activities (dating, visiting friends, "hanging out") predicted an increased rate of delinquency, whereas enrollment in organized and adult-supervised activities (work on the school newspaper, organized sports) predicted a decreased rate of delinquency. There is also some evidence that persons who return to a criminal lifestyle shortly after their release from prison do so on the strength of the belief that they have "nothing to lose" (Shover, 1983). Constructing a social bond with significant others, if not with conventional society, provides the individual with "something to lose," thereby augmenting his or her chances of remaining crime-free in the community (Cusson & Pinsonneault, 1986; Shover, 1983).

Choice-Based Change Strategies

The two primary features of choice behavior directly amenable to intervention are options and decision making. The goal of lifestyle intervention with reference to the options function of choice-based change strategies is to enlarge the client's fund of available options. This can be accomplished, in part, through the dissemination of information and the teaching of skills that expand a client's repertoire of feasible alternatives. The goal of lifestyle intervention with respect to the decision-making function of choice-based change strategies is to reinforce and broaden the client's decision-making competence by strengthening his or her resolve to evaluate thoroughly various life options and alternatives.

Option Expansion

Option-expanding intervention techniques are designed to augment a client's repertoire of options, alternatives, and possibilities. This is normally accomplished through skill development.

Lateral Thinking Skills

Psychologists commonly partition thinking into its convergent and divergent forms. Convergent or vertical thinking consists of a paring down of options and alternatives as a means of arriving at an optimal solution. Divergent or lateral thinking, on the other hand, entails expanding the range of contingencies and options by considering as many different potential solutions as possible. Edward de Bono (1977) offers several techniques designed to enhance a participant's lateral thinking or creativity skills. One such technique involves having the client generate alternative perceptions, descriptions, and interpretations of selected stimuli, such as geometric shapes and figures, altered or ambiguous photographs, and written stories. De Bono also utilizes practical exercises to teach clients how to suspend judgment, restructure perceptual patterns, and challenge accepted concepts. Although there is a dearth of long-term outcome data currently available on de Bono's lateral thinking program, he reports some success in using the program to improve the institutional behavior of incarcerated delinquents (de Bono, 1981).

Social Skills

Researchers have linked social skills deficits to problem drinking (Hover & Gaffney, 1991), illicit drug use (Linquist, Lindsay, & White, 1979), and criminal behavior (Freedman, Rosenthal, Donahoe, Schlundt, & McFall, 1978). Spence and Marzillier (1981) ascertained that offenders were less proficient in certain social skill areas—establishing eye contact and initiating conversations with strangers—than were nonoffenders. Social skills training (SST) might therefore be an alternative or adjunct to traditional therapy by virtue of its ability to expand the client's options in specific social contexts. Studies assessing this possibility have found SST capable of producing favorable outcomes in both alcohol abusers (Eriksen, Bjornstad, & Gertestam, 1986) and juvenile offenders (Sarason & Sarason, 1981). However, although short-term changes in targeted social skills (Twentyman, Jensen, & Kloss, 1978) and institutional behavior (Hollin, Huff, Clarkson, & Edmondson, 1982) have been recorded, there is little evidence of long-term reductions in criminal recidivism (Hollin & Henderson, 1984) or drug use (Hawkins, Catalano, Gillmore, & Wells, 1989).

Life Skills

Managing money, shopping for food, and conducting a job search are all skills most people take for granted. However, for those previously committed to a drug or criminal lifestyle, the prospect of having to balance a checkbook or secure an apartment can be genuinely frightening. Life skills training may help prepare clients for life in the community by providing them with a greater wealth of options. Oregon's Cornerstone program, for instance, instructs drug-involved offenders in basic work, food preparation, money management, and nutritional skills (Field, 1985). Treatment staff also encourage clients to develop leisure-time interests as a replacement for drug-based rituals. Pre-/posttesting of the various Cornerstone educational modules has revealed increased knowledge and social/occupational skills as a consequence of participation in the program, but has yet to address the program's long-term benefits, if indeed there are any (Field, 1985). A recent literature review, however, finds life skills training effective in reducing cigarette smoking, marijuana use, and problem drinking in junior high school students for periods of up to three years (Dusenbury & Botvin, 1992).

Educational Skills

A. Walsh (1985) reports that offenders who earned a general high school equivalency diploma (GED) as a condition of parole were significantly less likely to be rearrested (16%) during a 3½-year period of follow-up than were parolees who failed to complete the program (32%) or offenders who were never required to enroll in the first place (44%). Most studies have found, however, that educational programs in prison may lead to academic benefits but rarely to long-term gains with respect to reduced recidivism (Linden & Perry, 1982). Enrolling an offender in a GED or college program in the absence of any real change in thinking and behavior probably accomplishes little more than creating a more educated criminal. Questions concerning the relationship between education and drinking and the value of educational enrichment programs in reducing alcohol abuse have also been raised (Mulford, 1970). However, there is evidence that positive outcomes are attainable if arrangements are made for transition to a community-based academic program (Seashore, Haberfield, Irwin, & Baker, 1976) and if training in problem solving, moral reasoning, and cognitive self-management accompanies the academic curriculum (Ayers, Duguid, Montague, & Wolowidnyk, 1980).

Occupational Skills

Research outcomes on the relapse-retarding effects of job training are mixed. For example, Smith (1980) determined that offenders participating in a work release program were significantly less likely to receive a new felony conviction in comparison with a group of nonparticipating offenders (26% versus 47%), but Anderson (1985) reports that a job training program had no appreciable effect on first-year recidivism rates, and Johnson and Goldberg (1983) were unable to discern an antirecidivism effect for a training program in which vocational training was combined with an Outward Bound experience. Research suggests that occupational skills training may produce the most favorable results with minority subjects, ostensibly because of their greater disadvantage in finding employment (Beck, 1981), and persons who have been committed to a drug or criminal lifestyle for extended periods of time, because they probably never acquired basic job and employment skills in the first place (Jeffrey & Woopert, 1974).

Competence Enhancement

Decisions can be made using a variety of different methods. The simplest, and perhaps most popular, method is to list and contrast the advantages (benefits) and disadvantages (costs) of each alternative. For persons interested in a more thorough cost-benefit analysis, it is possible to weigh the likely consequences of a particular course of action by assigning a numerical value to the perceived significance of each consequence. Take, for instance, a woman who states she wants to stop smoking but whose assessment of the enjoyment of smoking (+15) outweighs her perceived negative consequences of continuing to smoke—sundry health considerations (−4), the financial cost of cigarettes (−3), and the social/interpersonal problems cigarette smoking can cause (−6). This not only illustrates why many clients relapse, but also reveals the limitations of a simple cost-benefit analysis of perceived outcomes. Nonetheless, the decision-making process can be improved, but it requires that individuals learn to give consideration to both priorities (values) and expectancies (goals).

Values-Based Intervention

Values have their foundation in early childhood experience, and parents and peers play a vital role in shaping a child's value system. Incidents occurring during adolescence and early adulthood, however, also influence value development. Agents of formal social control (school authorities, police, the courts) can exert particularly powerful effects on the organization and expression of values. Placing negative social sanctions on normative experimental drug use, for example, may actually promote, rather than inhibit, future drug use by encouraging the labeled adolescent to adopt a deviant value system in order to cope with feelings of social alienation and rejection (Kaplan, Johnson, & Bailey, 1986). The adoption of antisocial values in reaction to the negative labels society assigns its youthful lawbreakers is envisioned as a precipitating cause of crime and delinquency escalation in some quarters (Elliott, Ageton, & Canter, 1979). Values would appear to be especially important in treatment planning, given that some scholars view interventions for drug use and crime to be largely a matter of values clarification and values reorientation (Bush, 1983).

Values clarification is a procedure that allows for the identification, exploration, and review of personal values as a way of defining one's priorities in life. This approach has been successfully implemented with school-age children faced with moral issues or dilemmas (Casemont, 1983), nurses involved in the treatment of AIDS patients (Farrell, 1987), and juveniles participating in a hospital-based program for dually diagnosed (psychiatric and physical) patients (Franklin, 1986). Linkenbach (1990) describes a values clarification program employed at the Colorado State University Center for Alcohol Education in which subjects are instructed in how they might actualize myriad life options and improve their decision-making competence. This is accomplished through treatment in a nonthreatening environment where empowerment and values reorientation are emphasized and powerlessness and anomie minimized. Using a more traditional model, Brown and Peterson (1990) discuss the implications of values reorientation and spirituality in the treatment of alcohol abuse problems. Values clarification appears to exert a potential mitigating effect on drug abuse and crime by helping to identify priorities, changing the strength of values that promote deviance, and reinforcing values that support desirable behavior (Rokeach, 1983).

Goal-Setting Intervention

Research confirms that impulsivity (Brook, Whiteman, Gordon, & Brook, 1983) and inadequate forethought or planfulness (Shedler & Block, 1990) are prognostic of future drug-related difficulties. Furthermore, delinquent children and adolescents given a choice between a small immediate reward and a larger delayed reward opt for the immediate reward to a significantly greater extent than do nondelinquent children and adolescents (Mischel, 1974). Wilson and Herrnstein (1985) refer to this as a person's time horizon, the development of which has its roots in the early parent-child relationship. Expectancies would appear to play a key role in the decision to use drugs and commit crime in light of the fact that the probability of a behavior such as drug use or crime is a complex function of the expected consequences of drinking or crime, the subjective value assigned each consequence, the anticipated probability that each consequence will occur, and the subjective expected immediacy of each consequence. The results of studies assessing the decision-making criteria used to effect a choice of drug abuse (Rohsenow, Beach, & Marlatt, 1978) or crime (Carroll, 1978) suggest that the negative consequences of drug- and crime-related activities are generally apportioned less weight than the positive consequences because they tend to be less immediate and therefore more difficult to anticipate.

Expectancies could theoretically be modified through reinforcement and extension of the individual's time horizon. The time horizon, as represented by a subject's willingness to delay gratification, evolves over time, so that as a child matures he or she becomes increasingly more willing to delay immediate gratification in exchange for a more satisfying future reward (Mischel, 1974). For some reason, complete understanding of which continues to elude investigators, the time horizons of drug-involved and delinquent children do not mature at the same rate as do the time horizons of more socially responsible children. This developmental lag may be the cause of deviance, a consequence of it, or both. What we do know is that a short time horizon corresponds with deviance, and many deviance-promoting resolutions, such as the decision to use or reuse drugs (Marlatt & Gordon, 1985), bring to bear a conflict between the positive immediate effects and the negative long-term consequences of such conduct. Expectancies as they are, the positive short-term effects of drug use and crime normally prevail over the negative long-term consequences of a drug or criminal lifestyle in persons harboring short time horizons.

A conceivable redress for impulsivity, an abbreviated time horizon, and a weak life direction are training in goal setting. In such training, an individual is taught to differentiate between short-, intermediate-, and long-term consequences and how to establish and work toward short-, intermediate-, and long-range goals. Intervention techniques designed to bolster the ability to resist temptation and delay gratification therefore figure prominently in programs dedicated to the development of goal-setting and goal-attainment skills. Role playing and modeling are also indispensable in the effective implementation of the goal-setting technique. Goal-setting interventions that clearly embrace role playing and behavioral rehearsal strategies have been found particularly efficacious in reducing the aggression of a group of male students referred by their teachers for disruptive and potentially violent behavior (Lochman, Burch, Curry, & Lampron, 1984). Investigating the function of modeling in teaching delay of gratification to juvenile offenders, Stumphauzer (1972) discerned that delinquents exposed to high delay models exhibited increased delay of gratification themselves.

Cognition-Based Change Strategies

Because drug and criminal lifestyles are supported, reinforced, and maintained by the cognitive styles discussed in Chapter 4, these patterns must be addressed through cognition-based intervention strategies such as self-regulation, cognitive reframing, and rational restructuring. Equally cogent for the purposes of relapse prevention is finding the proper mental attitude for change.

The Attribution Triad

Attribution is a process whereby an individual draws causal inferences about another person's motives and intentions from observation of that person's behavior. People also make attributions about their own behavior. Lifestyle theory proposes a system of three interrelated attributions known as the *attribution triad,* which is viewed to be a cognitive precondition for change. It is hypothesized that persons lacking any portion of this triad will possess insufficient motivation or confidence to commence, let alone complete, the change process. The attribution triad is composed of a belief in the necessity of change, a belief in the possibility of change, and a belief in one's ability to effect change.

Belief in the Necessity of Change

Before a person can change his or her behavior, that individual must acknowledge that a problem exists and must take responsibility for solving that problem. Lifestyle theorists recognize that conditions outside one's personal control contribute to the onset and exacerbation of problem situations. However, the individual must accept full responsibility for his or her role in the problem and must labor to rectify the thoughts, behaviors, and feelings that often frustrate the change process. These issues speak directly to the "assignment of blame" component of the attribution triad, which finds its expression in a belief in the necessity of change. If people blame the balance of their problems on external factors (other people's actions, nefarious environmental conditions, bad luck), they will possess insufficient motivation to change their behavior. In fact, such persons typically conclude that it is their environment, not themselves, that needs modification. Reality would dictate, however, that we come to grips with our responsibilities as a prerequisite of behavioral change.

From the perspective of lifestyle theory, the development of a belief in the necessity of change requires the helping professional and client to work through a three-step procedure. The first step is for the practitioner to educate the client about choice and personal responsibility. Once this has been accomplished, the next step is for the practitioner to demonstrate to the client that despite the wide variety of problem situations the client has encountered in his or her life, there is one factor that has been common to all of these problems—that is, the client. Therefore, if the client desires that change take place, he or she must accept responsibility for his or her own role in the development and continuation of these problems. The third step is for the professional to challenge thinking patterns used by the client that minimize personal responsibility—mollification and sentimentality in particular. It is crucial that the therapist lay bare the irrational and self-defeating roots of these thinking patterns and help the client work toward the goal of rational thinking and constructive behavior. Though none of these steps is guaranteed to inspire a belief in the necessity of change, they can be helpful in establishing the proper conditions for an evolving sense of personal responsibility.

Belief in the Possibility of Change

Like a belief in the necessity of change, belief in the possibility of change is a precondition for cognitive and behavioral change. Simply holding to the conviction that one is responsible for a particular problematic behavior will have little bearing on future treatment outcomes if one does not also believe that change is theoretically possible and personally attainable. The first two components of the attribution triad are nonetheless complementary. Fisher and Farina (1979), for instance, report that patients furnished a biological or genetic interpretation of a problem behavior were much less likely to cope constructively with the problem and its future consequences than were patients provided a social learning interpretation. It is also worth noting that subjects receiving treatment for insomnia are better able to avoid relapse if they are led to attribute improvement to their own actions (relaxation training and time management) rather than to an optimal dose of sleeping medication (Davison, Tsujimoto, & Glaros, 1973). Likewise, subjects receiving intrinsic self-help training in smoking cessation made fewer external attributions for success and remained abstinent longer than did subjects treated solely or principally with nicotine gum (Harackiewicz, Sansone, Blair, Epstein, & Manderlink, 1987).

The possibility of change can be illustrated succinctly using Ellis's (1962) rational emotive imagery technique. After instructing the client to visualize a recent situation in which he or she felt angry, depressed, or fearful and having the client rate this feeling on a scale from 1 to 10 (1 representing a very low level of emotion and 10 a high level), the therapist guides the client down the scale, one rung at a time, until he or she reaches the bottom of the scale (i.e., level 1). Once this has been accomplished, the therapist asks the client if he or she was able to descend the scale successfully and, if so, to what the client attributes his or her success. The most common explanation provided by clients who have successfully completed this task (and most are capable of moving down at least four or five levels) is that they negotiated it by changing their thinking. This illustrates both the possibility of change and fact that thinking or cognition is one avenue through which change might be realized. The practitioner might also reinforce a belief in the possibility of change by having the client speak with others who have successfully exited a drug or criminal lifestyle.

Belief in One's Ability to Effect Change

A person may realize both the necessity and possibility of change and still not be in a position to change because of a lack of confidence in his or her ability to do so. This particular branch of the attribution triad derives from Albert Bandura's (1977) work on self-efficacy, a concept he defines as a person's perceived confidence in his or her ability to cope with a specific prospective situation. The situational specificity of the self-efficacy concept is portrayed in the results of a study by Rist and Watzl (1983), in which subjects recording low self-efficacy scores in alcohol-related situations displayed a higher rate of relapse than did subjects claiming robust self-efficacy in these same situations. However, self-efficacy for non-alcohol-related situations failed to correspond to a propensity for relapse. It has also been noted that self-efficacy is most strongly correlated with relapse during the first several months of the posttreatment period (Rychtarik, Prue, Rapp, & King, 1992).

Research on self-efficacy as an intervention for conduct-disordered behavior, delinquency, and crime is less extensive than research exploring the use of self-efficacy in the treatment of substance abuse problems, but what has been done up to this point is generally supportive of self-efficacy theory. Perry, Perry, and Rasmusson (1986), for instance, determined that a group of aggressive elementary school children reported greater self-efficacy in performing aggressive behaviors and lower self-efficacy in situations requiring their inhibition of aggressive impulses than did nonaggressive children. Failing to enlist support for the self-efficacy hypothesis with aggressive adolescent males, Elizabeth Cuddy and Cynthia Frame (1991) witnessed concordance between positive outcome expectancies and aggressiveness but no relationship when self-efficacy and aggressiveness were cross-lagged in group of aggressive and nonaggressive middle school boys.

The first step for therapists teaching self-efficacy to clients is to obtain an accurate measure of this particular cognitive precondition for change. Once areas of low self-efficacy have been identified, the next step is to provide remediation. Goldfried and Robins (1982) describe cognitive strategies potentially capable of enhancing self-efficacy, and Marlatt and Gordon (1985) review ways in which self-efficacy might be reinforced in persons who have been committed to a drug lifestyle. Marlatt and Gordon's recommendations include forming a working alliance with the client, breaking tasks down into manageable units so that the client can experience success, avoiding the willpower argument (i.e., drug abuse and criminal activity are consequences of a weak will) in favor of a focus on skill development, and providing the client with a steady stream of feedback and positive reinforcement.

Self-Regulation

It has been implied that substance abusers and ex-offenders who lack the ability to self-monitor their behavior, regulate their impulses, and maintain goal-oriented attitudes are at increased risk for relapse (Miller, 1991). Self-regulation and self-control would therefore appear to be potentially viable vehicles of cognitive-behavioral intervention. Training in self-regulation normally embodies such techniques as stimulus control, self-monitoring, self-reward, and self-punishment (Emmelkamp, 1986). Rate control, setting limitations, modification of social relationships, and other self-regulation procedures have been found effective in reducing alcohol consumption and alcohol-related problems in college students (Werch, 1990) and young adult felons (McMurran & Whitman, 1990). Given that self-monitoring has been known to effect behavioral change by focusing the individual's attention on the behavior in question (Emmelkamp, 1986), it may be a particularly promising technique if used as an adjunct to other cognitive-behavioral procedures and strategies.

Cognitive Reframing

Cognitive reframing is a clinical technique designed to shift a client's perception or interpretation of an event, situation, or person. As such, it is one way in which a practitioner might intervene in the case of historical-developmental conditions. In other words, although it may not be possible to change an event that has already transpired, it is possible to modify or reframe an individual's view of that event. Cognitive reframing is particularly popular with therapists who work with families. Extending family-based cognitive reframing procedures to the problem of delinquency, Alexander, Waldron, Barton, and Mas (1989) assert that negative attributions are more characteristic of families that raise one or more delinquent offspring than of families producing well-adjusted children. Alexander and his colleagues contend that effective family intervention requires the reframing of family problems and issues in an effort to shift the focus away from a seemingly incorrigible juvenile to transactions occurring within the family that give rise to acting-out behavior on the part of that juvenile.

Preparing the client for the possibility of future lapses and reinterpreting these slips as predictable experiences that should elicit a coping response rather than despair or frustration can also be conceptualized as a form of cognitive reframing. Marlatt and Gordon (1985) maintain that when lapses are reattributed to external, unstable, specific, controllable factors, the risk of relapse is substantially reduced. Investigations have shown that preparing clients for lapses and slips and reframing these lapses and slips as learning experiences can lower the rate of relapse in both alcohol abusers (Rodin, 1976) and heroin addicts (McAuliffe & Ch'ien, 1986). Of course, this approach is not foolproof; if misused, it can actually precipitate a relapse. Hence reframing lapses and slips as manageable problems may reduce the probability of relapse in persons committed to behavioral change. However, such reframing may arm clients who are less than fully committed to the change process with justification for using drugs or engaging in crime at some point in the future. For this reason, the therapist should use such an approach judiciously, and only after he or she has some sense of the client's motivation for change.

Cognitive Restructuring

As opposed to cognitive reframing, where the emphasis is on shifting perspective or relabeling a situation, cognitive restructuring involves a reconfiguration of thought content, expectancies, and assumptions so as to disrupt the eight thinking patterns that support a drug or criminal lifestyle. Though cognitive restructuring has been found effective in addressing problems of both drug (Oei & Jackson, 1982) and criminal (Ruby, 1984) natures, there is a need for as much structure as possible in the utilization of such a procedure. Maultsby (1975) provides such structure by listing five questions that can be used by clients to determine whether a particular thought, belief, or idea meets certain criteria for rationality:

1. Does it meet with objective reality?
2. Does it serve to protect the client's life and health?
3. Does it lead the client to achieve long- and short-term goals?
4. Does it help the client avoid conflict with others?
5. Does it make the client feel the way he or she wants to feel?

If at least three of these questions can be answered in the affirmative, then the belief is said to be rational. In earlier work, I applied these five questions to the eight thinking styles described in Chapter 4, and discovered that all eight fell well short of rationality as measured by Maultsby (Walters, 1990). In fact, most failed to satisfy even a single one of these five criteria for rational thinking.

Conclusion

Although surface differences may exist between drug and criminal lifestyles, the manner in which treatment is carried out with clients from these two groups deviates only slightly. This is because the current-contextual conditions, choices, and cognitive thinking patterns that contribute to a drug lifestyle dovetail with the current-contextual conditions, choices, and cognitive patterns that define a criminal lifestyle. What is more, there is a massive amount of crossover between these two lifestyles—that is, many individuals are simultaneously committed to both lifestyles or bounce back and forth between the two. It is also not uncommon to find lifestyle transformation as epitomized by the thinking of someone who stops using drugs only to start selling them. As the fundamental decisions and cognitive patterns differ only marginally between lifestyles, it is easy to see how an individual can go from being addicted to drugs to being addicted to selling drugs. Consequently, treatment approaches that focus on the problem area, be it drugs or crime, will tend to be less effective than procedures that address the underlying lifestyles and themes that link these two sets of behaviors. Treatment should therefore proceed along the lines of lifestyle overlap, crossover, and transfer, focusing on treatment issues common to both problem areas.

6. The Drug-Crime Connection Reconsidered

One of the primary objectives of a scientific piece of work is to take a thesis or idea and develop it to the point of advancing knowledge on a particular subject or issue. In this text I have introduced and examined the possibility that drug abuse and criminal activity constitute overlapping lifestyles linked by a common or related set of current-contextual conditions, choices, cognitions, and change strategies. Though lacking a definitive conclusion on the etiology, development, and amelioration of deviant behavior, there is ample evidence to suggest the presence of a robust, though variable, relationship between drugs and crime. Accordingly, drugs may cause crime in one situation, be a consequence of crime in a second situation, and be completely unrelated to crime under a third set of conditions. Another possibility, and one that finds preliminary support in the present investigation, is that drug abuse and crime are joined by commonalities in the lifestyles that support both.

One way of assessing a theory's worth might be to gauge its ability to predict relationships not currently observed and to establish goals and procedures for change. The degree to which a theory successfully forecasts future events and relationships is a measure of its utility from a research-analytic point of view. The extent to which it allows for clarity of expression, continuity of assessment and treatment, and construction of effective intervention strategies is an estimate of its clinical utility. A theory should consequently be judged on its merits—namely, its utility to researchers and clinicians—because more ephemeral criteria, such as the theory's relationship to "absolute truth," are unrealistic and unattainable. Moreover, as Heisenberg and Einstein observed in the physical sciences, truth and knowledge are relative concepts that vary according to how they are construed and measured. Lifestyle theory, like other theories that have been advanced over the years to explain the drug-crime connection, should therefore be evaluated against a criterion of usefulness.

A feature of the lifestyle model that speaks to its utility is the unified explanation it offers for drug abuse, crime, and the drug-crime connection. Drug abuse and criminal activity are conceptualized as overlapping lifestyles that, although distinct, are nonetheless bound by a common set of current-contextual conditions, choices, cognitions, and change strategies. Historical-developmental conditions, the focus of most traditional perspectives on the drug-crime connection, not only fail to explain drug-crime overlap, but in many cases show opposing patterns for these two forms of deviant behavior. This implies that although many of the factors that place a person at risk for future drug or criminal outcomes differ initially, the lifestyles that evolve from participation in drug use and criminal activity exhibit a converging pattern over time, perhaps because of the commonality in choices and cognitions that support both lifestyles. Thus developmental issues, in which the drug and criminal lifestyles appear to follow similar patterns of progression (see Walters, 1990, 1992a), are also of interest to researchers investigating the nature of the drug-crime connection.

Emotions and motivations are other constituents of lifestyle theory that are potentially capable of advancing our knowledge about the drug-crime question. Existential fear would appear to be one such factor. In lifestyle theory, existential fear is seen as the primary motivating force behind human behavior and the development of a drug or criminal lifestyle. Existential fear, which makes its appearance at birth, is experienced by the neonate as a primitive fear of nonexistence. This soon spills over into other areas of a young child's life and often inspires the expression of related fears, such as fear of abandonment, change, failure, commitment, and responsibility. The individual nevertheless has a choice: He or she may master existential fear through self-discipline or strive to escape this fear by retreating into a drug, criminal, or other lifestyle. Most people exhibit a combination of these two patterns, the relative importance of each defining a person's unique style of behavioral adjustment.

Lifestyle theory purports to assist the individual by acknowledging the presence of existential fear and reinforcing the individual's adaptive resources. Adaptation is awarded a prominent place in lifestyle theory by virtue of the fact that it serves as the antithesis of a drug or criminal lifestyle. Lifestyle theory defines adaptation as the modification of one's behavior in accordance with new information derived from one's interaction with the environment. Thinking plays a key role in this process, in that effective adaptation presumes a balance of values and expectancies. This contrasts sharply with a drug or criminal lifestyle, in which hedonistic values and short-term expectancies predominate. The paradox is that the longer the individual hides from existential fear through drug or criminal lifestyle involvement, the stronger the fear becomes, though its expression is often disguised. The reader's understanding of adaptability and its relationship to existential fear and deviant behavior might be assisted by a brief review of Jean Piaget's (1963) work on assimilation and accommodation.

Piaget theorized that early cognitive and moral skills unfold as a consequence of a child's interaction with his or her environment. *Assimilation* and *accommodation* are the terms Piaget used to explain this interactive relationship. According to Piaget, a young child learns by adapting existing mental representations or schemas to new information and situations. Assimilation involves the absorption or incorporation of new information into an existing schema (e.g., hairy four-legged animals that bark are assimilated into the schema dog). Accommodation occurs when the child confronts information that he or she cannot fully understand using an existing schema, and then modifies an existing cognitive structure to accommodate, integrate, and understand the new experience (e.g., encountering a hairy four-legged animal that purrs encourages the development of a new schema, cat). For Piaget, human cognitive development exists as an ongoing series of assimilations and accommodations that enhance the individual's adaptive resources by reinforcing his or her cognitive capabilities. Environmental change is consequently vital to future cognitive maturation in that it provides the subject with new learning experiences and the opportunity to develop his or her adaptive resources.

Lifestyle theory asserts that assimilation and accommodation are ways in which the individual manages his or her existential fear of change and uncertainty. Some persons attempt to master this fear by adapting to their environment; others handle the fear by escaping into lifestyle routines of predetermined roles and reactions. Someone who takes the adaptation/mastery route assimilates new information into existing schemas and accommodates his or her thinking to data for which no schema currently exists. This, in turn, reinforces the person's adaptive resources by expanding his or her sphere of knowledge and repertoire of skills and options. At the other extreme are persons who manage their fear by retreating into a drug or criminal lifestyle. Here the individual continues assimilating new information into existing schemas, but, because of low accommodation, distorts experiences and perceptions in order to fit them into preexisting cognitive sets. Because a lifestyle furnishes an individual with established rules, roles, relationships, and criteria for success and failure, it serves as an alternative to adaptive living, though in the end it leaves the individual even more vulnerable to existential fear and its derivatives.

Most children learn to manage their fear by engaging in role play and fantasy. In fact, these actions can be seen as adaptive in young children or preadolescents. However, given a supportive base of operations (secure attachment), adequate behavioral self-control (moderate sensation-seeking tendencies), and a reasonable degree of self-confidence (positive self-image), most children eventually abandon role play and fantasy as their principal avenues of problem management in favor of personal responsibility and adaptive living. There are, most assuredly, numerous conditional factors—person, situational, and interactive—capable of influencing a person's decision to either master or run from the existential fear of change. Personal choice variables, however, should not be overlooked. Lifestyle theory contends that although we may not be free to choose the conditions of our lives, we are free to adopt particular attitudes toward these conditions and to implement strategies designed to limit the effects these conditions have on our behavior.

To understand lifestyle theory is to realize that this is an evolving system subject to confusion and misinterpretation. Some of this can be attributed to the fact that the lifestyle concept was incompletely developed in several of the earlier writings on this subject, in that the original focus was on the lifestyle criminal or drug abuser as a real-life entity. Unfortunately, many professionals continue to think along these lines and do not understand that lifestyle theory currently conceives of lifestyles—drug, criminal, or otherwise—as caricatures that few people achieve in the absolute. Just as cartoon caricatures of politicians and celebrities exaggerate prominent physical characteristics of the persons being lampooned, so the concept of drug and criminal lifestyles magnifies the behavioral features of deviant activities. To avoid any further confusion, I have eliminated the terms *lifestyle drug abuser* and *lifestyle criminal* from this text and replaced them with descriptive analogues (e.g., persons committed to a drug lifestyle, individuals engaged in criminal lifestyle activities). It is a person's relative distance from the drug or criminal ideal, not whether he or she embodies all features of the caricature, that defines that person's commitment to a drug or criminal lifestyle.

The principal reason a drug or criminal lifestyle exists as a caricature rather than as a real-life entity is that, like any lifestyle, it is guided by specific roles and rules that no one could possibly follow without deviation. Some people, however, are more clearly committed to this ideal than others, and this is represented pictorially by the subject's relative distance from the caricature (see Figure 6.1). Lifestyle theory delineates the boundaries of lifestyle allegiance by drafting an arbitrary circle around the caricature and classifying subjects falling within this circle as significantly committed to the lifestyle ideal. It is imperative that the reader keep in mind, however, that lifestyle theory takes a dynamic view of human behavior and holds that a subject's distance from the ideal is constantly changing. This occurs as a consequence of the push and pull of forces that draw the individual toward the ideal (i.e., the reinforcing and gratifying aspects of a drug or criminal lifestyle) and the person's own efforts at self-control and avoidance of lifestyle activities. Persons situated in the overlapping zone between the drug and criminal lifestyles (see Figure 6.1) are said to be simultaneously committed to the drug and criminal lifestyle ideals.

Conclusion

The results of this inquiry into the nature of the drug-crime connection indicate that (a) the relationship between drug abuse and crime is genuine, meaningful, and quantifiable; and (b) there are three pathways through which this relationship is expressed. The most commonly cited, though not necessarily most heavily traversed, pathway between drug abuse and crime emanates from situations in which drug use causes crime, by loosening inhibitions,

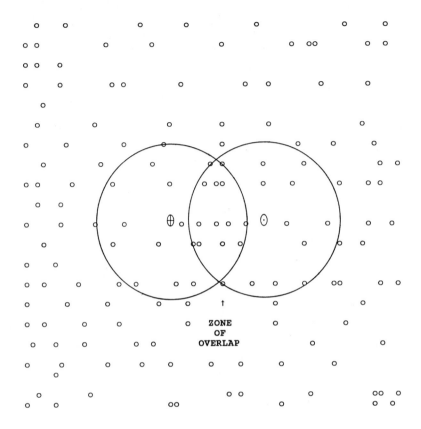

⊕ drug lifestyle caricature

⊘ criminal lifestyle caricature

o individual subjects

Figure 6.1. The Overlap Between Drug and Criminal Lifestyles

distorting judgment, fostering criminal associations, or creating a "need" for money. The second pathway of drug-crime overlap runs from crime to drugs and occurs in situations where crime expands a person's drug use opportunities through the provision of increased access to money, neutralization of stabilizing forces such as life structure, or extrication from conventional social controls.

The third pathway through which the drug-crime connection is expressed involves a reciprocal interaction of drug and criminal lifestyle issues. Instead of existing as a direct causal link, like the two previously mentioned pathways, the reciprocal route of overlap between drug abuse and crime arises from the interactive nexus that forms between these two forms of social deviance. Even though surface differences may exist between the drug and criminal lifestyles, the supporting themes, rituals, and thinking patterns are clearly related. Hence, although initial risk factors, as represented by research on historical-developmental conditions, may differ for drug abuse and crime, the drug-crime connection grows as a person's commitment to one or the other of these two lifestyles grows. For the sake of accuracy, Figure 6.1 should be portrayed in three-dimensional space, with an expanding zone of overlap between the drug and criminal lifestyles as the subject's commitment to either lifestyle begins to unfold. The future of lifestyle theory therefore rests with its ability to explain the underlying lifestyle that ties together many forms of socially deviant and nondeviant behavior and serves as an alternative to adaptation in response to existential fear.

References

Abel, G. G., & Annon, J. S. (1982, April). *Reducing deviant sexual arousal through satiation*. Workshop presented at the 4th National Conference on Sexual Aggression, Denver, CO.

Adler, F. (1983). *Nations not obsessed with crime*. Littleton, CO: Fred B. Rothman.

Agar, M. H. (1973). *Ripping and running: A formal ethnography of urban heroin addicts*. New York: Academic Press.

Agnew, R., & Petersen, D. M. (1989). Leisure and delinquency. *Social Problems, 36,* 332-350.

Ahmed, S. W., Bush, P. J., Davidson, F. R., & Ionnotti, R. J. (1984). *Predicting children's use and intentions to use abusable substances*. Paper presented at the annual meeting of the American Psychological Association, Washington, DC.

Ainslie, G. (1982). *Beyond microeconomics: Conflict among interests in a multiple self as a determinant of values*. Paper presented at the Conference on the Multiple Self, Paris.

Ainsworth, M. D. S. (1979). Infant-mother attachment. *American Psychologist, 34,* 932-937.

Akers, R. L. (1984). Delinquent behavior, drugs, and alcohol: What is the relationship? *Today's Delinquent, 3,* 19-47.

Akers, R. L. (1985). *Deviant behavior: A social learning approach* (2nd ed.). Belmont, CA: Wadsworth.

Alexander, J. F., Waldron, H. B., Barton, C., & Mas, C. H. (1989). The minimizing of blaming attributions and behaviors in delinquent families. *Journal of Consulting and Clinical Psychology, 57,* 19-24.

Anderson, A. (1985). Impact of a job training program on CETA-qualified probationers. *Federal Probation, 49,* 17-20.

Anderson, C. A., & Anderson, D. C. (1984). Ambient temperature and violent crime:
Tests of the linear and curvilinear hypotheses. *Journal of Personality and Social
Psychology, 46,* 91-97.

Andrucci, G. L., Archer, R. P., Pancoast, D. L., & Gordon, R. A. (1989). The
relationship of MMPI and sensation-seeking scales to adolescent drug use.
Journal of Personality Assessment, 53, 253-266.

Anglin, M. D., & Speckart, G. (1988). Narcotics and crime: A multisample, mul-
timethod analysis. *Criminology, 26,* 197-233.

Archer, D., & Gartner, R. (1984). *Violence and crime in cross-national perspective.* New
Haven, CT: Yale University Press.

Ayers, D. J., Duguid, S., Montague, C., & Wolowidnyk, S. (1980). *Effects of the
University of Victoria program: A post-release study.* Report prepared for the
Ministry of the Solicitor General of Canada, Ottawa.

Ball, J. C., Rosen, L., Flueck, J. A., & Nurco, D. N. (1981). The criminality of heroin
addicts: When addicted and when off opiates. In J. A. Inciardi (Ed.), *The
drugs-crime connection* (pp. 39-65). Beverly Hills, CA: Sage.

Bancroft, J. (1970). A comparative study of aversion and desensitization in the
treatment of homosexuality. In L. E. Burns & J. L. Worley (Eds.), *Behavior
therapy in the 1970's* (pp. 1-22). Bristol: John Wright.

Bandura, A. (1977). *Social learning theory.* Englewood Cliffs, NJ: Prentice Hall.

Barrett, M. E., Joe, G. W., & Simpson, D. D. (1990). Availability of drugs and
psychological proneness in opioid addiction. *International Journal of the Addictions, 25,* 1211-1226.

Bates, J. E., Maslin, C. A., & Frankel, K. A. (1985). Attachment security, mother-
child interaction, and temperament as predictors of behavior-problem ratings
at age three years. *Monographs of the Society for Research in Child Development,
50*(1-2, Serial No. 209).

Beck, J. L. (1981). Employment, community treatment center placement, and
recidivism: A study of released federal offenders. *Federal Probation, 45,* 3-8.

Becker, G. S. (1968). Crime and punishment: An economic approach. *Journal of
Political Economy, 76,* 169-217.

Bell, R. Q. (1979). Parent, child, and reciprocal influences. *American Psychologist, 34,*
821-826.

Bennett, T. (1986). A decision-making approach to opioid addiction. In D. B.
Cornish & R. V. Clarke (Eds.), *The reasoning criminal: Rational choice perspectives on offending* (pp. 83-103). New York: Springer-Verlag.

Bennett, T., & Wright, R. (1985). *The drug taking careers of English opiate addicts.*
Paper presented at the annual meeting of the American Criminological Society,
San Diego, CA.

Benson, M. L. (1985). Denying the guilty mind: Accounting for involvement in a
white-collar crime. *Criminology, 23,* 583-607.

Berndt, T. J., & Berndt, E. G. (1975). Children's use of motives and intentionality
in person perception and moral judgement. *Child Development, 46,* 904-912.

Biddle, B. J., Bank, B. J., & Marlin, M. M. (1980). Social determinants of adolescent
drinking. *Journal of Studies on Alcohol, 41,* 215-241.

Biernacki, P. (1990). Recovering from opiate addiction without treatment: A summary. *NIDA Research Monograph Series, 98,* 113-119.

Bishop, D. M. (1984). Deterrence: A panel analysis. *Justice Quarterly, 1,* 311-328.

Black, W. A., & Gregson, R. A. (1973). Time perspective, purpose in life, extroversion and neuroticism in New Zealand prisoners. *British Journal of Social and Clinical Psychology, 12,* 50-60.

Blakey, R., & Baker, R. (1980). An exposure approach to alcohol abuse. *Behaviour Research and Therapy, 18,* 319-325.

Blehar, M. C., Lieberman, A. F., & Ainsworth, M. D. S. (1977). Early face-to-face interaction and its relation to later infant-mother attachment. *Child Development, 48,* 182-194.

Block, J. (1971). *Lives through time.* Berkeley, CA: Bancroft.

Bohman, M., Cloninger, C. R., Sigvardsson, S., & von Knorring, A.-L. (1982). Predisposition to petty criminality in Swedish adoptees: I. Genetic and environmental heterogeneity. *Archives of General Psychiatry, 39,* 1233-1241.

Bradley, B. P., Phillips, G., Green, L., & Gossop, M. (1989). Circumstances surrounding the initial lapse to opiate use following detoxification. *British Journal of Psychiatry, 154,* 354-359.

Brecher, M., Wang, B. W., Wong, H., & Morgan, J. P. (1988). Phencyclidine and violence: Clinical and legal issues. *Journal of Clinical Psychopharmacology, 8,* 397-401.

Brier, S. S., & Fienberg, S. E. (1980). Recent economic modeling of crime and punishment: Support for the deterrence hypothesis? In S. E. Fieberg & A. J. Reiss (Eds.), *Indicators of crime and criminal justice: Quantitative studies* (pp. 82-97). Washington, DC: Government Printing Office.

Brook, J. S., Whiteman, M., Gordon, A. S., & Brook, D. W. (1983). Paternal correlates of adolescent marijuana use in the context of the mother-son and parental dyads. *Genetic Psychology Monographs, 108,* 197-213.

Brown, B. B., & Altman, I. (1983). Territoriality, defensible space and residential burglary: An environmental analysis. *Journal of Environmental Psychology, 3,* 203-220.

Brown, H. P., & Peterson, J. H. (1990). Rationale and procedural suggestions for defining and actualizing spiritual values in the treatment of dependency. *Alcoholism Treatment Quarterly, 7,* 17-46.

Brown, S. A., Goldman, M. S., Inn, A., & Anderson, L. R. (1980). Expectations of reinforcement from alcohol: Their domain and relation to drinking patterns. *Journal of Consulting and Clinical Psychology, 41,* 419-426.

Brunswick, A. F. (1988). Drug use and affective distress: A longitudinal study of urban black youth. *Advances in Adolescent Mental Health, 3,* 101-125.

Bry, B. H., McKeon, P., & Pandina, R. J. (1982). Extent of drug use as a function of number of risk factors. *Journal of Abnormal Psychology, 91,* 273-279.

Buikhuisen, W., Bontekoe, E. H. M., Plas-Korenhoff, C., & van Buuren, S. (1984). Characteristics of criminals: The privileged offender. *International Journal of Law and Psychiatry, 7,* 301-313.

Bureau of Justice Statistics. (1983a). *Prisoners and alcohol.* Washington, DC: Author.

Bureau of Justice Statistics. (1983b). *Prisoners and drugs.* Washington, DC: Author.

Burt, M. R. (1983). Justifying personal violence: A comparison of rapists and the general public. *Victimology, 8,* 131-150.

Bush, J. (1983). Criminality and psychopathology: Treatment for the guilty. *Federal Probation, 47,* 44-49.

Cadoret, R. J., & Cain, C. (1980). Sex differences in predictors of antisocial behavior in adoptees. *Archives of General Psychiatry, 37,* 941-951.

Cadoret, R. J., O'Gorman, T. W., Troughton, E., & Heywood, E. (1985). Alcoholism and antisocial personality: Interrelationships, genetic and environmental factors. *Archives of General Psychiatry, 42,* 161-167.

Cadoret, R. J., Troughton, E., O'Gorman, T. W., & Heywood, E. (1986). An adoption study of genetic and environmental factors in drug abuse. *Archives of General Psychiatry, 43,* 1131-1136.

Cahalan, C., & Room, R. (1974). *Problem drinking among American men.* New Brunswick, NJ: Rutgers Center for Alcohol Studies.

Cahalan, D., & Cisin, I. H. (1976). Epidemiological and social factors associated with drinking problems. In R. E. Tarter & A. A. Sugarman (Eds.), *Alcoholism: Interdisciplinary approaches to an enduring problem* (pp. 523-572). New York: Plenum.

Carr, R. R., & Meyers, E. J. (1980). Marijuana and cocaine: The process of change in drug policy. In Drug Abuse Council, *The facts about drug abuse* (pp. 153-189). New York: Free Press.

Carroll, J. S. (1978). A psychological approach to deterrence: The evaluation of crime opportunities. *Journal of Personality and Social Psychology, 36,* 1512-1520.

Casemont, W. (1983). Values clarification, Kohlberg and choosing. *Counseling and Values, 27,* 130-140.

Cernkovich, S. A., & Giordano, P. C. (1987). Family relationships and delinquency. *Criminology, 25,* 295-321.

Chaney, E. F., O'Leary, M. R., & Marlatt, G. A. (1978). Skill training with alcoholics. *Journal of Consulting and Clinical Psychology, 46,* 1092-1104.

Chein, I., Gerard, D. L., Lee, R. S., & Rosenfeld, E. (1964). *The road to H: Narcotics, delinquency, and social policy.* New York: Basic Books.

Christiansen, B. A., & Goldman, M. S. (1983). Alcohol-related expectancies versus demographic/background variables in the prediction of adolescent drinking. *Journal of Consulting and Clinical Psychology, 51,* 249-257.

Christiansen, B. A., Goldman, M. S., & Inn, A. (1982). Development of alcohol-related expectancies in adolescents: Separating pharmacological from social-learning influences. *Journal of Consulting and Clinical Psychology, 50,* 336-344.

Christiansen, B. A., & Teahan, J. E. (1987). Cross-cultural comparisons of Irish and American adolescent drinking practices and beliefs. *Journal of Studies on Alcohol, 48,* 558-562.

Cimler, E., & Beach, L. R. (1981). Factors involved in juveniles' decisions about crime. *Criminal Justice and Behavior, 8,* 275-286.

Cinquemani, D. K. (1975). *Drinking and violence among Middle American Indians.* Unpublished doctoral dissertation, Columbia University.

Clayton, R. R., & Voss, H. L. (1981). *Young men and drugs in Manhattan: A causal analysis.* Rockville, MD: National Institute on Drug Abuse.

Cloninger, C. R. (1987). Neurogenetic adaptive mechanisms in alcoholism. *Science, 236,* 410-416.

Cloninger, C. R., Bohman, M., & Sigvardsson, S. (1981). Inheritance of alcohol abuse: Cross-fostering analysis of adopted men. *Archives of General Psychiatry, 38,* 861-868.

Cohen, L. E., & Felson, M. (1979). Social change and crime rate trends: A routine activity approach. *American Sociological Review, 44,* 588-608.

Connell, D. B. (1976). *Individual differences in attachment: An investigation into stability, implications, and relationships to the structure of early language development.* Unpublished doctoral dissertation, Syracuse University.

Cook, P. J. (1980). Research on criminal deterrence: Laying the groundwork for the second decade. In N. Morris & M. Tonry (Eds.), *Crime and justice: An annual review of research* (Vol. 2, pp. 211-268). Chicago: University of Chicago Press.

Corbin, R. M. (1980). Decisions that might not get made. In T. S. Wallsten (Ed.), *Cognitive processes in choice and decision behavior.* Hillsdale, NJ: Lawrence Erlbaum.

Critchlow, B. (1986). The powers of John Barleycorn: Beliefs about the effects of alcohol on social behavior. *American Psychologist, 41,* 751-764.

Cromwell, P. F., Olson, J. N., Avary, D. W., & Marks, A. (1991). How drugs affect decisions by burglars. *International Journal of Offender Therapy and Comparative Criminology, 35,* 310-321.

Crowley, T. J. (1988). Learning and unlearning drug abuse in the real world: Clinical treatment and public policy. *NIDA Research Monograph Series, 84,* 100-121.

Cuddy, M. E., & Frame, C. (1991). Comparison of aggressive and nonaggressive boys' self-efficacy and outcome expectancy beliefs. *Child Study Journal, 21,* 135-152.

Cullen, F. T., Larson, M. T., & Mathers, R. A. (1985). Having money and delinquent involvement: The neglect of power in delinquency theory. *Criminal Justice and Behavior, 12,* 171-192.

Cummings, C., Gordon, J. R., & Marlatt, G. A. (1980). Relapse: Strategies of prevention and prediction. In W. R. Miller (Ed.), *The addictive behaviors.* Oxford: Pergamon.

Cushman, P. (1974). Detoxification of rehabilitated methadone patients: Frequency and predictors of long term success. *American Journal of Drug and Alcohol Abuse, 1,* 393-408.

Cusson, M., & Pinsonneault, H. P. (1986). The decision to give up crime. In D. Cornish & R. Clarke (Eds.), *The reasoning criminal: Rational choice perspectives on offending* (pp. 72-82). New York: Springer-Verlag.

Cynn, V. E. H. (1992). Persistence and problem-solving skills in young male alcoholics. *Journal of Studies on Alcohol, 53,* 57-62.

Dalby, J. T. (1985). Criminal liability in children. *Canadian Journal of Criminology, 27,* 137-145.

Daly, M., & Burton, R. (1983). Self-esteem and irrational beliefs: An exploratory investigation with implications for counseling. *Journal of Counseling Psychology, 30,* 361-366.

Davidson, R., & Schwartz, G. (1976). The psychobiology of relaxation and related states: A multi-process theory. In D. I. Mostofsky (Ed.), *Behavior control and the modification of physiological activity.* Englewood Cliffs, NJ: Prentice Hall.

Davison, G. C., Tsujimoto, R., & Glaros, A. (1973). Attribution and the maintenance of behavior change in falling asleep. *Journal of Abnormal Psychology, 82,* 124-135.

de Bono, E. (1977). *Lateral thinking: A textbook of creativity.* Markham: Penguin.

de Bono, E. (1981). *CoRT thinking program.* Toronto: Pergamon.

de Lint, J. (1976). The etiology of alcoholism with specific reference to sociocultural factors. In M. W. Everett, J. O. Waddell, & D. B. Heath (Eds.), *Cross-cultural approaches to the study of alcohol: An introductory perspective* (pp. 323-339). Paris: Mouton.

del Porto, J. A., & Masur, J. (1984). The effects of alcohol, THC, and diazepam in two different social settings: A study with human volunteers. *Research Communications in Psychology, Psychiatry, and Behavior, 9,* 201-212.

Denney, M. R., Baugh, J. L., & Hardt, H. D. (1991). Sobriety outcome after alcoholism treatment with biofeedback participation: A pilot inpatient study. *International Journal of the Addictions, 26,* 335-341.

Denoff, M. S. (1988). An integrated analysis of the contributions made by irrational beliefs and parental interaction to adolescent drug abuse. *International Journal of the Addictions, 23,* 655-669.

Dishion, T. J., Stouthamer-Loeber, M., & Patterson, G. R. (1984). *The monitoring construct* (OSLC technical report). (Available from OSLC, 207 East 5th, Suite 202, Eugene, OR 97401)

Dobinson, I., & Ward, P. (1986). Heroin and property crime: An Australian perspective. *Journal of Drug Issues, 16,* 249-262.

Doctor, R. M., & Polakow, R. L. (1973, August). *A behavior modification program for adult probationers.* Paper presented at the annual meeting of the American Psychological Association, Montreal.

Donovan, J. E., & Jessor, R. (1985). The structure of problem behavior in adolescence and young adulthood. *Journal of Consulting and Clinical Psychology, 53,* 890-904.

Douds, A. F., Engelsjord, M., & Collingwood, T. R. (1977). Behavior contracting with youthful offenders and their parents. *Child Welfare, 56,* 409-417.

Drafters, R., & Anderson, G. (1982). Conditioned tolerance to the tachycardia effect of ethanol in humans. *Psychopharmacology, 78,* 365-367.

Dusenbury, L., & Botvin, G. J. (1992). Substance abuse prevention: Competence enhancement and the development of positive life options. *Journal of Addictive Diseases, 11,* 29-45.

Eck, J. E., & Riccio, L. J. (1979). Relationship between reported crime rates and victimization survey results: An empirical and analytical study. *Journal of Criminal Justice, 7,* 293-308.

Eckerman, W. C., Bates, J. D., Rachal, J. V., & Poole, W. K. (1971). *Drug usage and arrest charges: A study of drug usage and arrest charges among arrestees in six metropolitan areas of the United States* (Final report BNDD Contract No. J-70-35). Washington, DC: Drug Enforcement Administration.

Egger, G. J., Webb, R. A. J., & Reynolds, I. (1978). Early adolescent antecedents of narcotic abuse. *International Journal of the Addictions, 13,* 773-781.

Einhorn, H. J., & Hogarth, R. M. (1978). Confidence in judgment: Persistence in the illusion of validity. *Psychological Review, 85,* 395-416.

Elliott, D. S., Ageton, S. S., & Canter, R. J. (1979). An integral theoretical perspective on delinquent behavior. *Journal of Research in Crime and Delinquency, 16,* 3-27.

Ellis, A. (1962). *Reason and emotion in psychotherapy.* New York: Lyle Stuart.

Emmelkamp, P. M. G. (1986). Behavior therapy with adults. In S. L. Garfield & A. E. Bergin (Eds.), *Handbook of psychotherapy and behavior change* (3rd ed., pp. 385-442). New York: John Wiley.

Emmelkamp, P. M. G., & Heeres, H. (1988). Drug addiction and parental rearing style: A controlled study. *International Journal of the Addictions, 23,* 207-216.

Erickson, P. G. (1976). Deterrence and deviance: The example of Canadian prohibition. *Journal of Criminal Law and Criminology, 67,* 222-232.

Eriksen, L., Bjornstad, S., & Gertestam, K. G. (1986). Social skills training in groups for alcoholics: One-year treatment outcome for groups and individuals. *Addictive Behaviors, 11,* 309-329.

Fagan, J., Weis, J. G., & Cheng, Y.-T. (1990). Delinquency and substance abuse among inner-city students. *Journal of Drug Issues, 20,* 351-402.

Fagan, J., & Wexler, S. (1987). Family origins of violent delinquents. *Criminology, 25,* 643-669.

Farley, F. (1986, May). The big T in personality. *Psychology Today,* pp. 44-52.

Farrell, B. (1987). AIDS patients: Values in conflict. *Critical Care Nursing Quarterly, 10,* 74-85.

Fattah, E. H. (1982). A critique of deterrence research with particular reference to the economic approach. *Canadian Journal of Criminology, 24,* 79-90.

Faupel, C. E. (1985). A theoretical model for socially oriented drug treatment policy. *Journal of Drug Education, 15,* 189-203.

Faupel, C. E. (1987). Heroin use and criminal careers. *Qualitative Sociology, 10,* 115-131.

Faupel, C. E., & Klockars, C. B. (1987). Drugs-crime connections: Elaborations from the life histories of hard-core heroin addicts. *Social Problems, 34,* 54-68.

Federal Bureau of Investigation. (1990). *Crime in the United States, 1989.* Washington, DC: Government Printing Office.

Feeney, F. (1986). Robbers as decision-makers. In D. B. Cornish & R. V. Clarke (Eds.), *The reasoning criminal: Rational choice perspectives on offending* (pp. 53-71). New York: Springer-Verlag.

Felson, M., & Cohen, L. E. (1977). *Criminal acts and community structure: A routine activity approach* (Working Paper in Applied Social Statistics). Urbana-Champaign: University of Illinois, Department of Sociology.

Felson, R. B., Ribner, S. A., & Siegel, M. S. (1984). Age and the effect of third parties during criminal violence. *Sociology and Social Research, 68,* 452-462.

Felson, R. B., & Steadman, H. J. (1983). Situational factors in disputes leading to criminal violence. *Criminology, 21,* 59-74.

Field, G. (1985). The cornerstone program: A client outcome study. *Federal Probation, 49,* 50-55.

Fillmore, K. M. (1988). *Alcohol use across the life course: A critical review of 70 years of international research.* Toronto: Addiction Research Foundation.

Finn, P. R., & Pihl, R. O. (1987). Men at high risk for alcoholism: The effect of alcohol on cardiovascular response to unavoidable shock. *Journal of Abnormal Psychology, 96,* 230-236.

Fisher, J. D., & Farina, A. (1979). Consequences of beliefs about the nature of mental disorders. *Journal of Abnormal Psychology, 88,* 320-327.

Franklin, D. (1986). A comparison of the effectiveness of values clarification presented as a personal computer system versus a traditional therapy group: A pilot study. *Occupational Therapy in Mental Health, 6,* 39-52.

Fraser, M. W., Hawkins, J. D., & Howard, M. O. (1988). Parent training for delinquency prevention. *Family Perspectives in Child and Youth Services, 11,* 93-125.

Freedman, B. J., Rosenthal, L., Donahoe, C. P., Schlundt, D. G., & McFall, R. M. (1978). A social behavioral analysis of skill deficits in delinquent and nondelinquent adolescent boys. *Journal of Consulting and Clinical Psychology, 46,* 1448-1462.

Friedman, A. S., Pomerance, E., Sanders, R., Santo, Y., & Utada, A. (1980). The structure and problems of the families of adolescent drug abusers. *Contemporary Drug Problems, 9,* 327-356.

Frykholm, B. (1979). Termination of the drug career: An interview study of 58 ex-addicts. *Acta Psychiatrica Scandinavica, 59,* 370-380.

Garofalo, J. (1987). Reassessing the lifestyle model of criminal victimization. In M. Gottfredson & T. Hirschi (Eds.), *Positive criminology* (pp. 23-42). Newbury Park, CA: Sage.

Gawin, F. H., & Ellinwood, E. H. (1988). Abstinence symptomatology and psychiatric diagnosis in cocaine abusers. *Archives of General Psychiatry, 43,* 107-113.

Gendreau, P., & Gendreau, L. P. (1970). The "addiction-prone" personality: A study of Canadian heroin addicts. *Canadian Journal of Behavioural Science, 2,* 18-25.

Gendreau, P., & Ross, R. R. (1987). Revivification of rehabilitation: Evidence from the 1980s. *Justice Quarterly, 4,* 349-407.

Gibbs, J. J., & Shelly, P. L. (1982). Life in the fast lane: A retrospective view by commercial thieves. *Journal of Research in Crime and Delinquency, 19,* 299-330.

Gibbs, J. P. (1975). *Crime, punishment, and deterrence.* New York: Elsevier.

Gillmore, M. R., Catalano, R. F., Morrison, D. M., Wells, E. A., Iritani, B., & Hawkins, J. D. (1990). Racial differences in acceptability and availability of drugs and early initiation of substance use. *American Journal of Drug and Alcohol Abuse, 16,* 185-206.

Giordano, P. C., Cernkovich, S. A., & Pugh, M. D. (1986). Friendships and delinquency. *American Journal of Sociology, 91,* 1170-1202.

Goldfried, M. R., & Robins, C. (1982). On the facilitation of self-efficacy. *Cognitive Therapy and Research, 6,* 361-380.

Goldman, F. (1981). Drug abuse, crime, and economics: The dismal limits of social choice. In J. A. Inciardi (Ed.), *The drugs-crime connection* (pp. 155-181). Beverly Hills, CA: Sage.

Goldsmith, H. H., Bradshaw, D. L., & Rieser-Danner, L. A. (1986). Temperamental dimensions as potential developmental influences on attachment. In J. V. Lerner & R. M. Lerner (Eds.), *New directions for child development: Temperament and psychosocial interaction in infancy and childhood* (pp. 5-34). San Francisco: Jossey-Bass.

Goldsmith, H. H., & Campos, J. J. (1982). Toward a theory of infant temperament. In R. N. Emde & R. J. Harmon (Eds.), *The development of attachment and affiliative systems* (pp. 161-193). New York: Plenum.

Goldstein, P. J. (1981). Getting over: Economic alternatives to predatory crime among street drug users. In J. A. Inciardi (Ed.), *The drugs-crime connection* (pp. 67-84). Beverly Hills, CA: Sage.

Goldstein, P. J. (1986). Homicide related to drug traffic. *Bulletin of the New York Academy of Medicine, 62,* 509-516.

Goodwin, D. W., Crane, B., & Guze, S. B. (1971). Felons who drink: An 8-year follow-up. *Quarterly Journal of Studies on Alcohol, 32,* 136-147.

Gould, L. C. (1969). Juvenile entrepreneurs. *American Journal of Sociology, 74,* 710-720.

Grant, B. F., Harford, T. C., & Grigson, M. B. (1988). Stability of alcohol consumption among youth: A national longitudinal survey. *Journal of Studies on Alcohol, 49,* 253-260.

Grasmick, H. G., & Green, D. E. (1980). Legal punishment, social disapproval and internalization as inhibitors of illegal behavior. *Journal of Criminal Law and Criminology, 71,* 325-335.

Green, B. T. (1981). An examination of the relationship between crime and substance abuse/use in a drug/alcohol treatment population. *International Journal of the Addictions, 16,* 627-645.

Guerra, N. G. (1989). Consequential thinking and self-reported delinquency in high-school youth. *Criminal Justice and Behavior, 16,* 440-454.

Hagnell, O., Lanke, J., Rorsman, B., & Ohman, R. (1986). Predictors of alcoholism in the Lundby study: II. Personality traits as risk factors for alcoholism. *European Archives of Psychiatry and Neurological Science, 235,* 192-196.

Hamlin, J. E. (1988). The misplaced role of rational choice in neutralization theory. *Criminology, 26,* 425-428.

Harackiewicz, J. M., Sansone, C., Blair, L. W., Epstein, J. A., & Manderlink, G. (1987). Attributional processes in behavior change and maintenance: Smoking cessation and continued abstinence. *Journal of Consulting and Clinical Psychology, 55,* 372-378.

Hare, R. D. (1978). Electrodermal and cardiovascular correlates of psychopathy. In R. D. Hare & D. Schalling (Eds.), *Psychopathic behavior* (pp. 107-144). New York: John Wiley.

Hare, R. D. (1982). Psychopathy and physiological activity during anticipation of an aversive stimulus in a distraction paradigm. *Psychophysiology, 19,* 266-271.

Hawkins, J. D., Catalano, R. F., Gillmore, M. R., & Wells, E. A. (1989). Skills training for drug abusers: Generalization, maintenance, and effects on drug use. *Journal of Consulting and Clinical Psychology, 57,* 559-563.

Henderson, M., & Hewstone, M. (1984). Prison inmate's explanations for interpersonal violence: Accounts and attributions. *Journal of Consulting and Clinical Psychology, 52,* 789-794.

Henningfield, J. E., & Goldberg, S. R. (1983). Control of behavior by intravenous nicotine injections in human subjects. *Pharmacology, Biochemistry and Behavior, 19,* 1021-1026.

Henshel, R. L., & Carey, S. (1975). Deviance, deterrence and knowledge of sanctions. In R. L. Henshel & R. A. Silverman (Eds.), *Perceptions in criminology* (pp. 54-73). New York: Columbia University Press.

Himle, D., Thyer, B., & Papsdorf, J. (1982). Relationships between rational beliefs and anxiety. *Cognitive Therapy and Research, 6,* 219-223.

Hirschi, T. (1969). *Causes of delinquency.* Berkeley: University of California Press.

Hirschi, T., & Gottfredson, M. (1983). Age and the explanation of crime. *American Journal of Sociology, 89,* 552-584.

Hollin, C. R., & Henderson, M. (1984). Social skills training with young offenders: False expectations and the "failure of treatment." *Behavioral Psychotherapy, 22,* 331-341.

Hollin, C. R., Huff, G. J., Clarkson, F., & Edmondson, A. E. (1982). *An evaluation of social skills training with young offenders in a borstal.* Paper presented at the International Conference on Psychology and the Law, Swansea, Wales.

Hook, J. G., & Cook, T. D. (1979). Equity theory and the cognitive ability of children. *Psychological Bulletin, 86,* 429-445.

Hough, M. (1987). Offenders' choice of target: Findings from victim surveys. *Journal of Quantitative Criminology, 3,* 355-369.

Hover, S., & Gaffney, L. R. (1991). The relationship between social skills and adolescent drinking. *Alcohol and Alcoholism, 26,* 207-214.

Hser, Y., Anglin, M. D., & McGlothlin, W. H. (1987). Sex differences in addict careers: I. Initiation of use. *American Journal of Drug and Alcohol Abuse, 13,* 33-57.

Hudleby, J. D. (1986). Personality and the prediction of delinquency and drug use. *British Journal of Criminology, 26,* 129-146.

Inciardi, J. A. (1979). Heroin use and street crime. *Crime & Delinquency, 25,* 335-346.

Inciardi, J. A., & Pottieger, A. E. (1991). Kids, crack, and crime. *Journal of Drug Issues, 21,* 257-270.

Irwin, J. (1970). *The felon.* Englewood Cliffs, NJ: Prentice Hall.

Jarvis, G., & Parker, H. (1989). Young heroin users and crime: How do the "new users" finance their habits? *British Journal of Criminology, 29,* 175-185.

Jeffrey, R., & Woopert, S. (1974). Work furlough as an alternative to incarceration: An assessment of its effects on recidivism and social cost. *Journal of Criminal Law and Criminology, 65,* 404-415.

Johnson, B. D., & Goldberg, R. T. (1983). Vocational and social rehabilitation of delinquents: A study of experimentals and controls. *Journal of Offender Counseling, Services and Rehabilitation, 6,* 43-60.

Johnson, R. E., Marcos, A. C., & Bahr, S. J. (1987). The role of peers in the complex etiology of adolescent drug use. *Criminology, 25,* 323-340.

Johnston, L. D., Bachman, J. G., & O'Malley, P. M. (1981). *Marijuana decriminalization: The impact on youth 1975-1980* (Monitoring the Future, Occasional Paper 13). Ann Arbor: University of Michigan, Institute of Social Research.

Kandel, D. B. (1978). Convergencies in prospective longitudinal surveys of drug use in normal populations. In D. B. Kandel (Ed.), *Longitudinal research on drug use: Empirical findings and methodological issues* (pp. 3-38). Washington, DC: Hemisphere-Wiley.

Kandel, D. B., & Adler, D. (1982). Socialization into marijuana use among French adolescents: A cross-cultural comparison with the U.S. *Journal of Health and Social Behavior, 23,* 295-309.

Kaplan, H. B., Johnson, R. J., & Bailey, C. A. (1986). Self-rejection and the explanation of deviance: Refinement and elaboration of a latent structure. *Social Psychology Quarterly, 49,* 110-128.

Kaplan, H. B., Martin, S. S., & Robbins, C. (1984). Pathways to adolescent drug use: Self-derogation, peer influence, weakening social control, and early substance use. *Journal of Health and Social Behavior, 25,* 270-289.

Katz, J. (1979). Concerted ignorance: The social construction of a cover-up. *Urban Life, 8,* 295-316.

Kazdin, A. E. (1985). *Treatment of antisocial behavior in children and adolescents.* Homewood, IL: Dorsey.

Kennedy, L. W., & Forde, D. R. (1990). Routine activities and crime: An analysis of victimization in Canada. *Criminology, 28,* 137-152.

Kernberg, O. F. (1972). Early ego integration and object relations. *Annals of the New York Academy of Sciences, 193,* 233-247.

Khatami, M., Mintz, J., & O'Brien, C. P. (1978). Biofeedback mediated relaxation in narcotic addicts. *Behavior Therapy, 9,* 968-969.

Kissin, B., Schenker, V., & Schenker, A. (1959). The acute effects of ethyl alcohol and chlorpromazine on certain physiological functions in alcoholics. *Quarterly Journal of Studies on Alcohol, 20,* 480-492.

Kitano, H. H. L., Chi, I., Rhee, S., Law, C. K., & Lubben, J. E. (1992). Norms and alcohol consumption: Japanese in Japan, Hawaii and California. *Journal of Studies on Alcohol, 53,* 33-39.

Larson, D. E., & Abu-Laban, B. (1968). Norm qualities and deviant drinking behavior. *Social Problems, 15,* 441-450.

Leigh, B. C. (1989). In search of the seven dwarves: Issues of measurement and meaning in alcohol expectancy research. *Psychological Bulletin, 105,* 361-373.

Lerner, M. J. (1970). The desire for justice and reactions to victims. In J. Macaulay & L. Berkowitz (Eds.), *Altruism and helping behavior: Social psychological studies of some antecedents and consequences* (pp. 205-229). New York: Academic Press.

Lewis, C. E., & Bucholz, K. K. (1991). Alcoholism, antisocial behavior and family history. *British Journal of Addiction, 86,* 177-194.

Lewis, C. E., Cloninger, C. R., & Pais, J. (1982). Sociopathy and alcoholism in a criminal population. *Alcoholism: Clinical and Experimental Research, 6,* 303.

Lewis, C. E., Rice, J. P., & Helzer, J. E. (1983). Psychiatric diagnostic interactions: Alcoholism and antisocial personality. *Journal of Nervous and Mental Disease, 171,* 105-113.

Linden, R., & Perry, L. (1982). The effectiveness of prison education programs. *Journal of Offender Counseling, Services and Rehabilitation, 6,* 43-57.

Linkenbach, J. (1990). Adlerian techniques for substance abuse prevention and intervention. *Individual Psychology: Journal of Adlerian Theory, Research, and Practice, 46,* 203-207.

Linquist, C. M., Lindsay, T. S., & White, G. D. (1979). Assessment of assertiveness in drug abusers. *Journal of Clinical Psychology, 35,* 676-679.

Lochman, J. E., Burch, P. R., Curry, J. F., & Lampron, L. B. (1984). Treatment and generalization effects of cognitive-behavioral and goal-setting interventions with aggressive boys. *Journal of Consulting and Clinical Psychology, 52,* 915-916.

Loeber, R. (1990). Development and risk factors of juvenile antisocial behavior and delinquency. *Clinical Psychology Review, 10,* 1-41.

Loftin, C., McDowall, D., & Boudouris, J. (1989). Economic change and homicide in Detroit, 1926-1979. In T. R. Gurr (Ed.), *Violence in America: Vol. 1. The history of crime* (pp. 163-177). Newbury Park, CA: Sage.

Ludwig, A. M. (1985). Cognitive processes associated with "spontaneous" recovery from alcoholism. *Journal of Studies on Alcohol, 46,* 53-58.

MacDonald, J. E., & Gifford, R. (1989). Territorial cues and defensible space theory: The burglar's point of view. *Journal of Environmental Psychology, 9,* 193-205.

Maddux, J. F., & Desmond, D. P. (1982). Residence relocation inhibits opioid dependence. *Archives of General Psychiatry, 39,* 1313-1317.

Maguire, K., & Flanagan, T. J. (1991). *Sourcebook of criminal justice statistics: 1990.* Washington, DC: Government Printing Office.

Main, M., Tomasini, L., & Tolan, W. (1979). Differences among mothers of infants judged to differ in security. *Developmental Psychology, 15,* 472-473.

Marcos, A. C., Bahr, S. J., & Johnson, R. E. (1986). Test of a bonding/association theory of adolescent drug use. *Social Forces, 65,* 135-161.

Marlatt, G. A. (1978). Craving for alcohol, loss of control, and relapse: A cognitive behavioral analysis. In P. C. Kendall & S. P. Hollon (Eds.), *Cognitive-behavioral interventions: Theory, research and procedures.* New York: Plenum.

Marlatt, G. A., & Gordon, J. R. (1980). Determinants of relapse: Implications for the maintenance of behavior change. In P. O. Davidson & S. M. Davidson (Eds.), *Behavioral medicine: Changing health lifestyles* (pp. 410-472). New York: Brunner/Mazel.

Marlatt, G. A., & Gordon, J. R. (Eds.). (1985). *Relapse prevention: Maintenance strategies in the treatment of addictive behaviors.* New York: Guilford.

Marlatt, G. A., & Marques, J. K. (1977). Meditation, self-control and alcohol abuse. In R. B. Stuart (Ed.), *Behavioral self-management: Strategies, techniques and outcomes.* New York: Brunner/Mazel.

Matsueda, R. L. (1988). The current state of differential association theory. *Crime & Delinquency, 34,* 277-306.

Maultsby, M. C. (1975). *Help yourself to happiness through rational self-counseling.* New York: Institute for Rational Living.

Mayhew, P. M., Clarke, R. V., Sturman, A., & Hough, J. M. (1976). *Crime as opportunity.* London: Her Majesty's Stationery Office.

McAuliffe, W. E., & Ch'ien, J. M. N. (1986). Recovery training and self-help: A relapse-prevention program for treated opiate addicts. *Journal of Substance Abuse Treatment, 3,* 9-20.

McBride, D. C., Burgman-Habermehl, C., Alpert, J., & Chitwood, D. D. (1986). Drugs and homicide. *Bulletin of the New York Academy of Medicine, 62,* 497-508.

McClelland, D. C., Davis, W. N., Kalin, R., & Wanner, R. (1972). *The drinking man: A theory of human motivation.* New York: Free Press.

McCord, J. (1988). Parental behavior in the cycle of aggression. *Psychiatry, 51,* 14-23.

McMurran, M., & Whitman, J. (1990). Strategies of self-control in male young offenders who have reduced their alcohol consumption without formal intervention. *Journal of Adolescence, 13,* 115-128.

Mednick, S. A., Gabrielli, W. F., & Hutchings, B. (1984). Genetic influences in criminal convictions: Evidence from an adoption cohort. *Science, 224,* 891-894.

Mednick, S. A., & Kandel, E. S. (1988). Congenital determinants of violence. *Bulletin of the American Academy of Psychiatry and the Law, 16,* 101-109.

Meier, R. F., & Johnson, W. T. (1977). Deterrence as social control: The legal and extralegal production of conformity. *American Sociological Review, 42,* 292-304.

Menard, S., & Huizinga, D. (1989). Age, period, and cohort size effects on self-reported alcohol, marijuana, and polydrug use: Results from the National Youth Survey. *Social Science Research, 18,* 174-194.

Meyer, R. E., & Mirin, S. M. (1979). *The heroin stimulus: Implications for a theory of addiction.* New York: Plenum.

Meyers, E. J. (1980). American heroin policy: Some alternatives. In Drug Abuse Council, *The facts about "drug abuse"* (pp. 190-247). New York: Free Press.

Miller, D., & Jang, M. (1977). Children of alcoholics: A 20-year longitudinal study. *Social Work Research Abstracts, 13,* 23-29.

Miller, L. (1991). Predicting relapse and recovery in alcoholism and addiction: Neuropsychology, personality, and cognitive style. *Journal of Substance Abuse Treatment, 8,* 277-291.

Ministry of Welfare, Health, and Cultural Affairs. (1985). *Policy on drug users.* Rijswijk, Netherlands: Author.

Mischel, W. (1974). Processes in delay of gratification. *Advances in Experimental Psychology, 7,* 249-292.

Moore, M. S. (1977). *Buy and bust.* Lexington, MA: Lexington.

Mulford, H. A. (1970). Education and drinking behavior. In G. L. Maddox (Ed.), *The domesticated drug: Drinking among collegians* (pp. 81-97). New Haven, CT: College & University Press.

Murphy, T. J., Pagano, R. R., & Marlatt, G. A. (1986). Lifestyle modification with heavy alcohol drinkers: Effects of aerobic exercise and meditation. *Addictive Behaviors, 11,* 175-186.

Nakken, C. (1988). *The addictive personality: Roots, rituals, and recovery.* Center City, MN: Hazelden.

Nathan, P. E. (1988). The addictive personality is the behavior of the addict. *Journal of Consulting and Clinical Psychology, 56,* 183-188.

Nelson, R. E. (1977). Irrational beliefs in depression. *Journal of Consulting and Clinical Psychology, 45,* 1190-1191.

Newcomb, M. D., & Bentler, P. M. (1988). *Consequences of adolescent drug use: Impacts on the lives of young adults.* Newbury Park, CA: Sage.

Newcomb, M. D., Fahy, B. N., & Skager, R. (1988). Correlates of cocaine use among adolescents. *Journal of Drug Issues, 18,* 327-354.

Newcomb, M. D., Maddahian, E., & Bentler, P. M. (1986). Risk factors for drug use among adolescents: Concurrent and longitudinal analyses. *American Journal of Public Health, 76,* 525-531.

Newman, O. (1972). *Defensible space: Crime prevention through urban design.* New York: Macmillan.

O'Brien, C. P., Childress, R., McLellan, T., & Ehrman, R. (1990). Integrating systematic cue exposure with standard treatment in recovering drug dependent patients. *Addictive Behaviors, 15,* 355-365.

O'Connor, L. E., Berry, J. W., Morrison, A., & Brown, S. (1992). Retrospective reports of psychiatric symptoms before, during, and after drug use in a recovering population. *Journal of Psychoactive Drugs, 24,* 65-68.

Oei, T. P. S., & Jackson, P. R. (1982). Social skills and cognitive behavioral approaches to the treatment of problem drinking. *Journal of Studies on Alcohol, 43,* 532-547.

Ogloff, J. R., & Wong, S. (1990). Electrodermal and cardiovascular evidence of a coping response in psychopaths. *Criminal Justice and Behavior, 17,* 231-245.

O'Neil, J. A. (1992). *Drug use forecasting: 1991 annual report.* Washington, DC: National Institute of Justice.

Orcutt, J. D. (1987). Differential association and marijuana use: A closer look at Sutherland (with a little help from Becker). *Criminology, 25,* 341-358.

Orsagh, T., & Witte, A. D. (1981). Economic status and crime: Implications for offender rehabilitation. *Journal of Criminal Law and Criminology, 72,* 1055-1071.

Osgood, D. W., Johnston, L. D., O'Malley, P. M., & Bachman, J. G. (1988). The generality of deviance in late adolescence and early adulthood. *American Sociological Review, 53,* 81-93.

Panella, D. H., Cooper, P. F., & Henggeler, S. W. (1982). Peer relations in adolescence. In S. W. Henggeler (Ed.), *Delinquency and adolescent psychopathology: A family ecological systems approach* (pp. 139-161). Littleton, MA: Wright-PSG.

Parker, H., & Newcombe, R. (1987). Heroin use and acquisitive crime in an English community. *British Journal of Sociology, 38,* 331-350.

Paternoster, R. (1987). The deterrent effect of the perceived certainty and severity of punishment: A review of the evidence and issues. *Justice Quarterly, 4,* 173-217.

Paternoster, R. (1989). Decisions to participate in and desist from four types of common delinquency: Deterrence and the rational choice perspective. *Law and Society Review, 23,* 7-40.

Paternoster, R., & Iovanni, L. (1986). The deterrent effect of perceived severity: A reexamination. *Social Forces, 64,* 751-777.

Patterson, G. R., & Dishion, T. J. (1985). Contributions of families and peers to delinquency. *Criminology, 23,* 63-79.

Pearson, F. S., & Weiner, N. A. (1985). Criminology: Toward an integration of criminological theories. *Journal of Criminal Law and Criminology, 76,* 116-150.

Perry, D. G., Perry, L. C., & Rasmusson, P. (1986). Cognitive social learning mediators of aggression. *Child Development, 57,* 700-711.

Phillips, L., & Votey, H. L. (1987). The influence of police interventions and alternative income sources on the dynamic process of choosing crime as a career. *Journal of Quantitative Criminology, 3,* 251-273.

Piaget, J. (1963). The attainment of invariants and reversible operations in the development of thinking. *Social Research, 30,* 283-299.

Pickens, R. W., & Svikis, D. S. (1988). The twin method in the study of vulnerability to drug abuse. *NIDA Research Monograph Series, 89,* 41-51.

Piliavin, I., Gartner, R., Thornton, C., & Matsueda, R. L. (1986). Crime, deterrence, and rational choice. *American Sociological Review, 51,* 101-119.

Pithers, W. D., Kashima, K., Cumming, G. F., Beal, L. S., & Buell, M. M. (1987). *Relapse prevention of sexual aggression.* Paper presented at the New York Academy of Sciences, New York.

Pithers, W. D., Marques, J. K., Gibat, C. C., & Marlatt, G. A. (1983). Relapse prevention with sexual aggressives: A self-control model of treatment and maintenance of change. In J. G. Greer & I. R. Stuart (Eds.), *The sexual aggressor: Current perspectives on treatment* (pp. 214-239). New York: Van Nostrand.

Quinsey, V. L., & Marshall, W. L. (1983). Procedures for reducing inappropriate sexual arousal. In J. G. Greer & I. R. Stuart (Eds.), *The sexual aggressor: Current perspectives on treatment* (pp. 267-289). New York: Van Nostrand.

Reitman, J. (1974). Without surreptitious rehearsal, information in short-term memory decays. *Journal of Verbal Learning and Verbal Behavior, 13,* 365-377.

Rist, F., & Watzl, H. (1983). Self-assessment of relapse risk and assertiveness in relation to treatment outcome of female alcoholism. *Addictive Behaviors, 8,* 121-127.

Robins, L. N., Davis, D. H., & Goodwin, D. W. (1974). Drug use by U.S. Army enlisted men in Vietnam: A follow-up on their return home. *American Journal of Epidemiology, 99,* 235-249.

Rodin, J. (1976). Density, perceived choice, and response to controllable and uncontrollable outcomes. *Journal of Experimental Social Psychology, 12,* 564-578.

Rohrer, J. H., & Edmonson, M. S. (Eds.). (1960). *The eighth generation: Cultures and personalities of New Orleans Negroes.* New York: Harper.

Rohsenow, D. J., Beach, L. R., & Marlatt, G. A. (1978, July). *A decision-theory model of relapse.* Paper presented at the summer conference of the Alcoholism and Drug Abuse Institute, University of Washington, Seattle.

Rohsenow, D. J., Monti, P. M., Zwick, W. R., Nirenberg, T. D., Liepman, M. R., Binkoff, J. A., & Abrams, D. B. (1989). Irrational beliefs, urges to drink and drinking among alcoholics. *Journal of Studies on Alcohol, 50,* 461-464.

Rokeach, M. (1983). A value approach to the prevention and reduction of drug abuse. *NIDA Research Monograph Series, 47,* 172-194.

Rokeach, M., & Ball-Rokeach, S. J. (1989). Stability and change in American value priorities. *American Psychologist, 44,* 775-784.

Rosenberg, M., Schooler, C., & Schoenbach, C. (1989). Self-esteem and adolescent problems: Modeling reciprocal effects. *American Sociological Review, 54,* 1004-1018.

Ross, S. (1973). A study of living and residence patterns of former heroin addicts as a result of their participation in a methadone treatment program. In *Proceedings of the Fifth National Conference on Methadone Treatment* (pp. 554-561). New York: National Association for the Prevention of Addiction to Narcotics.

Rowe, D. C., & Gulley, B. L. (1992). Sibling effects on substance use and delinquency. *Criminology, 30,* 217-233.

Ruby, C. T. (1984). Defusing the hostile ex-offender: Rational behavior training. *Emotional First Aid, 1,* 17-22.

Rutter, M., Yule, B., Quinton, D., Rowlands, O., Yule, W., & Berger, M. (1975). Attainment and adjustment in two geographical areas: III. Some factors accounting for area differences. *British Journal of Psychiatry, 126,* 520-533.

Rychtarik, R. G., Prue, D. M., Rapp, S. R., & King, A. C. (1992). Self-efficacy, aftercare and relapse in a treatment program for alcoholics. *Journal of Studies on Alcohol, 53,* 435-440.

Sarason, I. G. (1968). Verbal learning, modeling, and juvenile delinquency. *American Psychologist, 23,* 254-266.

Sarason, I. G., & Sarason, B. R. (1981). Teaching cognitive and social skills to high school students. *Journal of Consulting and Clinical Psychology, 49,* 908-918.

Sarbin, T. R., Allen, V. L., & Rutherford, E. E. (1965). Social reinforcement, socialization, and chronic delinquency. *British Journal of Social and Clinical Psychology, 4,* 179-184.

Schimerman, S. R. (1974). *Project evaluation report: Operation identification.* St. Louis, MO: Law Enforcement Assistance Council.

Schonfeld, L., Rohrer, G. E., Dupree, L. W., & Thomas, M. (1989). Antecedents of relapse and recent substance use. *Community Mental Health Journal, 25,* 245-249.

Schuckit, M. A. (1987). Biological vulnerability to alcoholism. *Journal of Consulting and Clinical Psychology, 55,* 301-309.

Seashore, M., Haberfield, S., Irwin, J., & Baker, K. (1976). *Prisoner education: Project Newgate and other college programs.* New York: Praeger.

Seattle Law and Justice Planning Office. (1975). *Burglary reduction program* (Final report prepared for the Law Enforcement Assistance Administration). Seattle, WA: Author.

Shannon, L. W. (1982). *Assessing the relationship of adult criminal careers to juvenile careers: A summary.* Washington, DC: Office of Juvenile Justice and Delinquency Prevention.

Shapiro, A. P., & Nathan, P. E. (1986). Human tolerance to alcohol: The role of Pavlovian conditioning processes. *Psychopharmacology, 88,* 90-95.

Shapiro, D. H., & Walsh, R. N. (Eds.). (1984). *Meditation: Classic and contemporary perspectives.* New York: Aldine.

Shedler, J., & Block, J. (1990). Adolescent drug use and psychological health: A longitudinal inquiry. *American Psychologist, 45,* 612-630.

Sheldon, W. (1954). *Atlas of men.* New York: Harper.

Sher, K. (1985). Subjective effects of alcohol: The influence of setting and individual differences in alcohol expectancies. *Journal of Studies on Alcohol, 46,* 137-146.

Shorkey, C., & Sutton-Smith, K. (1983). Reliability and validity of the Rational Behavior Inventory with a clinical population. *Journal of Clinical Psychology, 39,* 34-38.

Shover, N. (1983). The later stages of ordinary property offender careers. *Social Problems, 31,* 208-218.

Siegel, R. A. (1978). Probability of punishment and suppression of behavior in psychopathic and nonpsychopathic offenders. *Journal of Abnormal Psychology, 87,* 514-522.

Siegel, R. K. (1984). Cocaine aroma in the treatment of cocaine dependence. *Journal of Clinical Psychopharmacology, 4,* 61-62.

Siegel, S. (1986). Environmental modulation of tolerance: Evidence from benzodiazepine research. In H. H. Frey, W. P. Koella, W. Forscher, & H. Meinardi (Eds.), *Tolerance to beneficial and adverse effects of antiepileptic drugs* (pp. 89-100). New York: Raven.

Siegel, S. (1988). Drug anticipation and the treatment of dependence. *NIDA Research Monograph Series, 84,* 1-24.

Siegel, S., Hinson, R. E., Krank, M. D., & McCully, J. (1982). Heroin "overdose" death: The contribution of drug-associated environmental cues. *Science, 216,* 436-437.

Silberman, C. E. (1978). *Criminal violence, criminal justice.* New York: Random House.

Simo, S., & Perez, J. (1991). Sensation seeking and antisocial behavior in a junior student sample. *Personality and Individual Differences, 12,* 965-966.

Simons, R. L., Conger, R. D., & Whitbeck, L. B. (1988). A multistage social learning model of the influences of family and peers upon adolescent substance abuse. *Journal of Drug Issues, 18,* 293-315.

Simons, R. L., & Robertson, J. F. (1989). The impact of parenting factors, deviant peers, and coping style upon adolescent drug use. *Family Relations, 38,* 273-281.

Simons, R. L., Robertson, J. F., & Downs, W. R. (1989). The nature of the association between parental rejection and delinquent behavior. *Journal of Youth and Adolescence, 18,* 297-310.

Simpson, D. D., & Marsh, K. L. (1986). Relapse and recovery among opioid addicts 12 years after treatment. *NIDA Research Monograph Series, 72,* 86-103.

Slovic, P., Fischoff, B., & Lichtenstein, S. (1977). Behavioral decision theory. *Annual Review of Psychology, 28,* 1-39.

Smith, G. T., Roehling, P. V., Goldman, M. S., & Christiansen, B. A. (1987, August). *Alcohol expectancies predict adolescent drinking: A longitudinal study.* Paper presented at the annual meeting of the American Psychological Association, Washington, DC.

Smith, R. R. (1980). Longitudinal behavioral assessment of work release. *Journal of Offender Counseling, Services and Rehabilitation, 5,* 31-39.

Smith, T., Houston, B., & Zurawski, R. (1984). Irrational beliefs and the arousal of emotional distress. *Journal of Counseling Psychology, 3,* 190-201.

Speckart, G., & Anglin, M. D. (1986). Narcotics use and crime: An overview of recent research advances. *Contemporary Drug Problems, 13,* 741-769.

Spence, S. H., & Marzillier, J. S. (1981). Social skills training with adolescent male offenders: II. Short term, long term, and generalized effects. *Behaviour Research and Therapy, 19,* 349-368.

Stabenau, J. R. (1986). Basic research on heredity and alcohol: Implications for clinical application. *Social Biology, 32,* 297-321.

Stall, R., & Biernacki, P. (1986). Spontaneous remission from the problematic use of substances: An inductive model derived from a comparative analysis of the alcohol, opiate, tobacco, and food/obesity literatures. *International Journal of the Addictions, 21,* 1-23.

Stephens, R. C., & Smith, R. B. (1976). *Copping and caveat emptor: The street addict as consumer.* New York: New York State Office of Drug Abuse Services, Bureau of Social Science Research.

Stermac, L. E., & Segel, Z. V. (1989). Adult sexual contact with children: An examination of cognitive factors. *Behavior Therapy, 20,* 573-584.

Stewart, J. K. (1986). The urban strangler: How crime causes poverty in the inner city. *Police Review, 37,* 6-10.

Stimson, G. V., & Oppenheimer, E. (1982). *Heroin addiction: Treatment and control in Britain.* London: Tavistock.

Strayer, D. L., & Kramer, A. R. (1990). Attentional requirements of automatic and controlled processing. *Journal of Experimental Psychology: Learning, Memory, and Cognition, 16,* 67-82.

Stumphauzer, J. S. (1972). Increased delay of gratification in young prison inmates through imitation of high delay peer models. *Journal of Personality and Social Psychology, 21,* 10-17.

Sutherland, E. H. (1939). *Principles of criminology* (3rd ed.). Philadelphia: J. B. Lippincott.

Sutherland, E. H., & Cressey, D. R. (1978). *Principles of criminology* (10th ed.). New York: Harper & Row.

Sutker, P. B., Moan, C. E., Goist, K. C., & Allain, A. N. (1984). MMPI subtypes and antisocial behaviors in adolescent alcohol and drug abusers. *Drug and Alcohol Dependence, 13,* 235-244.

Sykes, G. M., & Matza, D. (1970). Techniques of delinquency. In M. E. Wolfgang, L. Savitz, & N. Johnston (Eds.), *The sociology of crime and delinquency* (2nd ed, pp. 292-299). New York: John Wiley.

Thompson, R. A. (1986). Temperament, emotionality, and infant cognition. In J. V. Lerner & R. M. Lerner (Eds.), *Temperament and social interaction in infants and children* (pp. 35-53). San Francisco: Jossey-Bass.

Thornberry, T. P. (1987). Toward an interactional theory of delinquency. *Criminology, 25,* 863-892.

Tittle, C. R., Burke, M. J., & Jackson, E. F. (1986). Modeling Sutherland's theory of differential association: Toward an empirical clarification. *Social Forces, 65,* 405-432.

Tittle, C. R., Villemez, W. J., & Smith, D. A. (1978). The myth of social class and criminality: An empirical assessment of the empirical evidence. *American Sociological Review, 43,* 643-656.

Tuchfeld, B. S. (1981). Spontaneous remission in alcoholics: Empirical observations and theoretical implications. *Journal of Studies on Alcohol, 42,* 626-641.

Twentyman, C. T., Jensen, M., & Kloss, J. D. (1978). Social skills training for the complex offender: Employment-seeking skills. *Journal of Clinical Psychology, 34,* 320-326.

Vaillant, G. E. (1983). *The natural history of alcoholism.* Cambridge, MA: Harvard University Press.

Vaillant, G. E., & Milofsky, E. S. (1982). Natural history of male alcoholism: IV. Paths to recovery. *Archives of General Psychiatry, 39,* 127-133.

Van Voorhis, P., Cullen, F. T., Mathers, R. A., & Garner, C. C. (1988). The impact of family structure and quality of delinquency: A comparative assessment of structural and functional factors. *Criminology, 26,* 235-261.

Venables, P. H. (1987). Autonomic nervous system factors in criminal behavior. In S. A. Mednick, T. E. Moffitt, & S. A. Stack (Eds.), *The causes of crime: New biological approaches* (pp. 110-136). New York: Cambridge University Press.

Venables, P. H., Mednick, S. A., Schulsinger, F., Raman, A. C., Bell, B., Dalais, J. C., & Fletcher, R. P. (1978). Screening for risk of mental illness. In G. Serban (Ed.), *Cognitive defects in development of mental illness* (pp. 273-303). New York: Brunner/Mazel.

Votey, H. L. (1986). Substance abuse and crime in Sweden: Econometric estimates of linkages. In P. Shapiro & H. L. Votey (Eds.), *Econometric analysis of crime in Sweden* (pp. 23-34). Rockville, MD: National Institute of Justice.

Waldo, G. P., & Chiricos, T. G. (1972). Perceived penal sanctions and self-reported criminality: A neglected approach to deterrence research. *Social Problems, 19,* 522-540.

Waldorf, D. (1976). Life without heroin: Some social adjustments during long-term periods of voluntary abstention. In R. H. Coobs, L. J. Fry, & P. G. Lewis (Eds.), *Socialization in drug abuse* (pp. 365-384). Cambridge, MA: Schenkman.

Walsh, A. (1985). An evaluation of the effect of adult basic education on rearrest rates among probationers. *Journal of Offender Counseling, Services and Rehabilitation, 9,* 69-76.

Walsh, D. P. (1978). *Shoplifting: Controlling a major crime.* London: Macmillan.

Walsh, D. (1986). Victim selection procedures among economic criminals: The rational choice perspective. In D. B. Cornish & R. V. Clarke (Eds.), *The reasoning criminal: Rational choice perspectives on offending* (pp. 39-52). New York: Springer-Verlag.

Walters, G. D. (1990). *The criminal lifestyle: Patterns of serious criminal conduct.* Newbury Park, CA: Sage.

Walters, G. D. (1992a). Drug-seeking behavior: Disease or lifestyle? *Professional Psychology: Research and Practice, 23,* 139-154.

Walters, G. D. (1992b). *Foundations of criminal science: Vol. 1. The development of knowledge.* New York: Praeger.

Walters, G. D. (1992c). A meta-analysis of the gene-crime relationship. *Criminology, 30,* 595-613.

Walters, G. D. (1994). The drug lifestyle: One pattern or several? *Psychology of Addictive Behaviors, 8*(1), 8-13.

Walters, G. D., & White, T. W. (1987). *Examining lifestyle criminality: The Leavenworth 500.* Unpublished manuscript, United States Penitentiary, Leavenworth, KS.

Walters, G. D., & White, T. W. (1989a). Heredity and crime: Bad genes or bad research? *Criminology, 27,* 455-485.

Walters, G. D., & White, T. W. (1989b). The thinking criminal: A cognitive model of lifestyle criminality. *Criminal Justice Research Bulletin, 4*(4).

Walters, G. D., & White, T. W. (1990). Attachment and social bonding in maximum and minimum security prison inmates. *American Journal of Criminal Justice, 15,* 54-69.

Warr, M., & Stafford, M. (1991). The influence of delinquent peers: What they think or what they do? *Criminology, 30,* 851-865.

Washton, A. M., & Gold, M. S. (1986). Recent trends in cocaine abuse: A view from the national hotline, "800-COCAINE." *Advances in Alcohol and Substance Abuse, 6,* 31-47.

Watts, W. D., & Wright, L. S. (1990). The relationship of alcohol, tobacco, marijuana, and other illegal drug use to delinquency among Mexican-American, black, and white adolescent males. *Adolescence, 25,* 171-181.

Weaver, F. M., & Carroll, J. S. (1985). Crime perceptions in a natural setting by expert and novice shoplifters. *Social Psychology Quarterly, 48,* 349-359.

Wells, L. E., & Rankin, J. H. (1988). Direct parental controls and delinquency. *Criminology, 26,* 263-285.

Werch, C. E. (1990). Behavioral self-control strategies for deliberately limiting drinking among college students. *Addictive Behaviors, 15,* 119-128.

Wermuth, L., & Scheidt, S. (1986). Enlisting family support in drug treatment. *Family Process, 25,* 25-33.

Werner, H. (1957). The concept of development from a comparative and organismic point of view. In D. Harris (Ed.), *The concept of development.* Minneapolis: University of Minnesota Press.

West, D. J. (1982). *Delinquency: Its roots, careers, and prospects.* Cambridge, MA: Harvard University Press.

West, D. J., & Farrington, D. P. (1973). *Who becomes delinquent?* London: Heinemann.

White, H. R., Johnson, V., & Garrison, C. G. (1985). Drug-crime nexus among adolescents and their peers. *Deviant Behavior, 6,* 183-204.

White, J. L., Moffitt, T. E., Earls, F., Robins, L., & Silva, P. A. (1990). How early can we tell? Predictors of childhood conduct disorder and adolescent delinquency. *Criminology, 28,* 507-533.

Wilkins, D. (1964). *Social deviance: Social policy, action and research.* London: Tavistock.

Wilson, J. Q., & Herrnstein, R. J. (1985). *Crime and human nature.* New York: Simon & Schuster.

Wood, M. D., Nagoshi, C. T., & Dennis, D. A. (1992). Alcohol norms and expectations as predictors of alcohol use and problems in a college student sample. *American Journal of Drug and Alcohol Abuse, 18,* 461-476.

Woody, G. E., O'Brien, C. P., & Rickels, K. (1975). Depression and anxiety in heroin addicts: A placebo-controlled study of doxepin in combination with methadone. *American Journal of Psychiatry, 132,* 447-450.

Yochelson, S., & Samenow, S. E. (1976). *The criminal personality: Vol. 1. A profile for change.* New York: Jason Aronson.

Zacny, J. P., Bodker, B. K., & de Wit, H. (1992). Effects of setting on the subjective and behavioral effects of d-amphetamine in humans. *Addictive Behaviors, 17,* 27-33.

Zinberg, N. E. (1984). *Drug, set, and setting: The basis for controlled intoxicant use.* New Haven, CT: Yale University Press.

Index

123

About the Author

Glenn D. Walters has spent the past two years as a staff psychologist and coordinator of the substance abuse program at the Federal Correctional Institute in Schuylkill, Pennsylvania, an adult male medium security federal prison. After receiving a B.A. in psychology from Lebanon Valley College in 1976, an M.A. in clinical psychology from Indiana University of Pennsylvania in 1978, and a Ph.D. in counseling psychology from Texas Tech University in 1982, he completed a one-year internship at Dwight David Eisenhower Army Medical Center in Fort Gordon, Georgia. Subsequent to his internship, he was assigned to the mental health directorate of the U.S. Disciplinary Barracks in Fort Leavenworth, Kansas, where he remained until his discharge from the military in August 1984. He then took a position with the Federal Bureau of Prisons, first at the United States Penitentiary in Leavenworth, Kansas, then at the Federal Correctional Institute in Fairton, New Jersey, and finally at the Federal Correctional Institution in Schuylkill. His current primary research interests include investigations into the genetic correlates of crime, attempts to improve criminal assessment, and extension of lifestyle theory to substance abuse, compulsive gambling, and other behaviors known to overlap with the criminal lifestyle.